DR. RUTH'S
GUIDE TO
COLLEGE LIFE

Also by Dr. Ruth K. Westheimer

The Art of Arousal
Dr. Ruth's Guide for Good Sex
All in a Lifetime
Heavenly Sex
Sex for Dummies
Grandparenthood
Dr. Ruth Talks about Grandparents
The Value of Family
Dr. Ruth's Pregnancy Guide for Couples
Surviving Salvation

DR. RUTH'S GUIDE TO COLLEGE LIFE

THE SAVVY STUDENT'S HANDBOOK

Dr. Ruth K. Westheimer and Pierre Lehu

MADISON BOOKS
Lanham • New York • Oxford

Published by Madison Books
4720 Boston Way
Lanham, Maryland 20706

12 Hid's Copse Road
Cumnor Hill, Oxford OX2 9JJ, England

Distributed by National Book Network

Library of Congress Cataloging-in-Publication Data

Westheimer, Ruth K. (Ruth Karola), 1928–
    Dr. Ruth's guide to college life : the savvy student's handbook / Dr. Ruth K.
Westheimer and Pierre Lehu.
      p. cm.
    Includes index.
    ISBN 1-56833-171-1 (pbk. : alk. paper)
    1. College student orientation—United States—Handbooks, manuals, etc.
2. College students—United States—Conduct of life—Handbooks, manuals,
etc. I. Title: Doctor Ruth's guide to college life. II. Title: Guide to
college life. III. Lehu, Pierre A. IV. Title.
  LB2343.32 .W47 2000
378.1'98—dc21   00-030532

Ben Zoma says: Who is wise? The one who learns from everyone, as it is written, "from all my teachers I have gotten understanding" (Psalm 119). *Pirkei Avot (The Sayings of the Fathers) 4:1*

To Nick and Brett

best wishes!

Dr. Ruth

Westheimer

CONTENTS

ACKNOWLEDGMENTS

Dr. Ruth K. Westheimer:
To the memory of my entire family who perished during the Holocaust. I am thankful that they had the opportunity to instill in me the much cherished values of the Jewish tradition before they were lost to me. To the memory of my late husband, Fred, who encouraged me in all my endeavors. Thanks to my family of now: daughter Miriam Westheimer, Ed.D., son-in-law Joel Einleger, M.B.A., their children Ari and Leora, my son Joel Westheimer, Ph.D., daughter-in-law Barbara Leckie, Ph.D., and their daughter Michal. The best grandchildren in the entire world!

Thanks to all the many family members and friends for adding so much to my life! An entire chapter would be needed to mention them all but some must be mentioned here: Pierre Lehu and I are now entering our twentieth year of working together—to the best "Minister of Communications" thank you and to many more years of cooperation! Cliff Rubin, my assistant—thanks! Ruth Bachrach, Rabbi Stephen Berkowitz, Susan Brown, Carlita C. de Chavez, Martin Englisher, Cynthia Fuchs Epstein, Ph.D., Howard Epstein, Yosh Gafni, Rachel Gilon, Ellen Goldberg, David A. Goslin, Ph.D., Fred Howard, Vera Jelinek, Richard Kandell, Alfred Kaplan, Steve Kaplan, Ph.D., Michael and Ronnie Kassan, Amy Kassiola, Joel Kassiola, Ph.D., Bonnie Kaye, Richard and Barbara Kendall, Cantor Michael Kruk, Marga and Bill Kunreuther, Marsha Lebby, Rabbi and Mrs. William

Lebeau, Joanne Lehu Esq., President Arthur Levine, Bill Levy, Lou Lieberman, Ph.D., and Mary Cuadrado, Ph.D., John and Ginger Lollos, Jonathan and Ruchy Mark, Dale Ordes, Henry and Sydelle Osterg, Robert Pinto, Fred and Anne Rosenberg, Simeon and Rose Schreiber, Romie and Blanche Shapiro, Amir Shaviv, John and Marianne Slade, Hannah Strauss, Greg Willenborg, and Ben Yagoda. And to all the people who worked so hard to bring this book to fruition at Madison Books, especially Jed Lyons, Rich Freese, Michael Dorr, Michael Messina, Alyssa Theodore, Lynn Gemmell, and Ginger Strader.

Pierre Lehu:

I would like to thank Dr. Sara Arthur, New York University, Greg Baird, North Central Michigan University, Eleanor Oi, SUNY Binghamton, and Dr. Ira Sacker, H.E.E.D., for their assistance in writing this book. I would also like to thank my parents for helping to put me through college, my wife, Joanne, whom I met while she was still in college, my children, Peter, who is in college, and Gabrielle, who's on her way, and Dr. Ruth, for sending me back to reminisce about my college days.

INTRODUCTION

Let's pretend that you are in my office and I've asked you to tell me what thoughts come to mind when I say the word "college." The first images might be ivy-covered walls, poster-covered dorm walls, and crowds cheering in a football stadium. Or maybe, if you're a little on the wild side, you might think of an "Animal House" beer blast or the naked midnight run at Princeton. But if you haven't spent much time in college yet, those images aren't really your own. They are only reflections of what you've seen in the media or heard about.

Had you been a graduate looking back on your college years, it wouldn't be the buildings or the stadium that would pop into your mind. It would be the multitude of people you interacted with—roommates, classmates, fraternity brothers, sorority sisters, faculty, and administration members. That's because going to college is not about having a new place to sleep and take classes (hopefully not at the same time!) but about being introduced to a new world of fascinating people.

One more person will emerge from your college years—a new you. Since the change will be gradual, you may not notice it, but those people you left behind—your parents, siblings, extended family, and friends—are sure to see the difference.

Dealing with all of these people, both new and old, is going to be a challenge. You'll be forming new relationships of all sorts while having to cope with the changes in your old relationships. Since you won't have a teacher to guide you or a textbook to study, you could run into some rough patches where you might be feeling lonely, confused, depressed, or D: All of the above. To help you find your way is why I've written this book.

While I may be best known for giving out frank advice about sex, and a sexual relationship or two is a good possibility considering you'll be spending four years mingling with thousands of other hot-blooded young people, I also help people solve relationship issues of all sorts. When I lecture at colleges and universities, which I do all the time, I get just as many questions about relationships as I do about sex, including those having to do with roommates and teachers. Eventually most people adapt, though not everybody does, but with the right advice, that adaptation process can go a lot smoother.

By the way, I'm not taking on this task by myself. I also want to say a word about my coauthor, Pierre Lehu. We've been working together for nineteen years, and some time before that fateful day we met he'd received a B.A. in politics and French and an M.B.A. in management. After working closely with me all these years, he deserves an honorary doctorate as a therapist. And that his son is a member of the college class of 2002 gives him special insight into the process.

Now, while I'm known for using words like penis, vagina, and masturbation with aplomb, I want you, and your parents, to know that basically I'm old-fashioned and a square. It's not that I'm not willing to try new things, but I've discovered that many of the values that were handed down to us by our parents and grandparents still work the very best, especially when it comes to how we relate to people. Love and loneliness, friendship and lust are all emotions that have been with us since the beginning of time, and while scientists may be able to invent some terrific new contraptions, they've yet to come up with any machine that will provide companionship or love. In fact, it's been shown that people who spend too much time on their computer supposedly looking for cyberfriendships wind up feeling even more lonely and depressed.

But luckily for you, you're about to spend four years surrounded by real live human beings, most of them your age, of both sexes, and sharing the same emotions that you have—excitement, curiosity, and sexual desire—and I expect these years to be the most wonderful imaginable. I expect you to make friendships that will last the rest of your life, especially with a little bit of help from me.

LEAVING HOME UNSCATHED

I am well aware that not every entering freshman is a recent high school graduate, leaving home for the first time. But it is those students who are going to have the biggest adjustments to make, and therefore I am directing much of my advice to them, particularly in this first chapter, which deals with separation. A sixty-year-old grandmother who decides to get her B.A. will have many obstacles to overcome, but leaving her parents for the first time won't be one of them.

How an individual reacts to the final snips at those apron strings depends on many factors but no one will escape completely unscathed. Even young people who swear they can't stand their parents, and who have spent the past few years fighting with them almost constantly, will still have some difficulties leaving home.

SEPARATION ANXIETY

You may have heard the term "separation anxiety" but if Psych 101 is still in the future for you, its meaning may be a little cloudy. Since I'm prone to feeling the effects of separation anxiety, I'll use myself as an example to illustrate what it means. When I was ten years old, my mother and grandmother put me on a train in Frankfurt bound for a school in Switzerland. Because of the Holocaust, that school became an orphanage for all of us sent there from Germany and I never saw my parents or grandparents again. Now, more than fifty years later, I still feel the repercussions of those events so that I always have some tension whenever I leave a loved one, even if I know I'm going to see them the next day. Obviously I developed my case under extreme circumstances, but we all can feel some anxiety when leaving someone whom we care about, especially if it's the very first time that we will be leaving home for an extended time.

You may be wondering how much separation anxiety a freshman leaving for college normally feels. Having stated the question, I now have to give you my little speech about the word "normal." I am constantly being asked by people what is the "normal" amount of this or that (most often the frequency of having sex, though penis size is a close second, and no, size does not matter). In some cases there are statistics from which you can find out the average, but I never give those statistics. Why not? Because the concept of normal doesn't apply in most of these instances. You can make a graph of human behavior and show that it falls along a bell curve, but just because your individual statistics don't put you right at the top of the curve doesn't mean that your life is automatically over. For example, if a person discovers that they are homosexual, obviously they are not statistically "normal." But can they change their sexual identity in an attempt to become "normal"? Not any more than a black person can change the color of skin, or a person who is extra tall, or extra short, like myself, can change height. Even if you are not very different from average, there still is not much you can do about it. If the average height for men in this country is 5′10″, and you're 5′8″, what choice do you have than to be your height? And the same principle applies to what you're feeling about going away to college.

Most freshmen have a certain amount of anxiety about leaving home. After they've spent the first seventeen or eighteen years of their life under that protective roof, that's to be expected. But if you notice that your level of discomfort seems higher than those exhibited by your friends, is that going to increase the chances that you are going to calm down? Of course not. It's going to make you feel worse, even though it shouldn't. Your feelings belong only to you, and it is irrelevant whether you are more worried or less worried than they are. And by the way, those friends of yours who say they can't wait to get away from home, don't believe them. Oh, they may like the idea of being on their own, but they're also worried about what college will be like. That's why I tell people not to compare themselves. It's your life and your feelings, and so you have to learn to deal with such feelings based strictly on your own emotional makeup and not on what the so-called "normal" reaction might be.

> **Q.** I was very excited when those letters came in accepting me to college, and after I made my choice, my parents drove me back to the campus so I could get a better look around, and everything I saw seemed to have a magical quality because I was going to be a part of it. Now it's only a couple of weeks before I have to leave, and I've been crying myself to sleep every night because I'm so afraid. I don't know if I'm going to be able to go through with this, though what could I possibly tell my family and friends if I chicken out?

> **A.** From your letter it sounds like you are keeping your fears to yourself. You seem to think that it is somehow wrong to be afraid so you don't want to admit it to anybody and you're only releasing those tears of yours in the dark. Don't assume that because you tell your parents, or anyone else, that you're afraid that it means you're going to have to drop out of college before you even get there. My guess is if you do tell people who love you, they'll be able to comfort you and make it easier for you to handle this experience.

What if you're very afraid? What if you're terrified? What if your stomach has been in a knot for the past month and each day that brings you closer to saying good-bye makes that knot seem bigger and tighter? Do you have to just tough it out? The answer is no. There are several things you can do. The first is to talk about it with someone. Keeping your feelings bottled up usually intensifies them. If you can express them to someone who'll listen sympathetically, you'll feel better. The first people you should go to are your parents, assuming that they're the sympathetic type. If they're not, or if you know they're very upset about your leaving and you don't want to make them even more worried by revealing your own emotional turmoil, then find someone else. How about your grandparents? Or an aunt or uncle you feel close to? Maybe an older sibling who's gone through the same thing? You may even have cousins currently in college who could share their experiences. And then there are your friends. Since they're probably feeling at least some of the same fears, they'll hear you out. If none of those options are available, or helpful, then go to see a professional counselor. It could be a religious leader. It could be the guidance counselor in your school. Or it could be a psychologist.

I know it's not that easy for a teenager to seek professional help. Many teens don't even like going to see a medical doctor. But if you were to cut yourself badly, wouldn't you see a doctor? If you had a toothache, wouldn't you go to the dentist? Of course you would. While our society doesn't always pay the same attention to psychological suffering, or pain, that it does to physical pain, such pains are not that dissimilar. In fact, psychological problems can sometimes cause physical pain, like one of those permanent knots that can take root in your stomach. Just like a medical doctor, a professional counselor can help you heal those psychological problems. So don't suffer needlessly; speak out and get the help you need.

TIPS

- If you're having problems dealing with your feelings about leaving home, write them down. Sometimes such a list can help you get a handle on what is disturbing you the most, and then you can perhaps come up with a solution.

- If you know any college students, make a point of talking to them. You don't have to tell them how you feel, but they'll be able to give you real answers to your questions, and that might be a big help.

TIPS

- If the college you are going to isn't very far away, ask your parents to take you there, or make the trip yourself. Now that you know you're going there, you can make some more practical investigations that may make you more comfortable. If you know what dorm you're going to be in, see if you can get inside and even take some pictures or videos.

WHAT ELSE YOU CAN DO TO CALM DOWN

Besides exercising your jaw muscles by talking about how you feel, there are other ways to calm yourself down. One of the great natural relaxants is to exercise your other muscles. It doesn't matter what you do, just as long as it gets your heart rate going and uses up some of that adrenaline that's coursing through your system. Maybe you could call your friends and organize a game of basketball or volleyball. You could go for a run or a bike ride or a long walk. Or maybe do some crunches or push-ups in your room. Just make sure to work some physical activity into your daily schedule.

Thanks in part to MTV, young people today seem to prefer entertainment activities that jump around, but if you're looking for a distraction to forget about a problem, it's better if you can really lose yourself in it. An excellent source of such "lost" time is a good book. If you've got several weeks ahead of you, pick up a series of books like Tolkien's trilogy, *The Lord of the Rings*, and lose your worries in that imaginary world. Whatever the book, find some that are easy to read and have a good story line that will enable you to dive into it and push reality into the background for a while.

I could list many other activities—going to the movies, playing games, cooking dinner for your family, going through all the family photo albums or home videos, cleaning out the garage or attic or your own closet. I'm sure you could come up with many more. The basic point is, don't just sit there slouched on the couch worrying about what college is going to be like. Life can't be rehearsed. There are some experiences you just have to *go through* in order to know what will happen, and worrying about them won't do you any good. So try to take your mind off these thoughts by focusing on something else.

YOUR PARENTS HAVE FEELINGS TOO

By the way, don't think you're the only one worried about your up-coming departure. You can be sure that your family, especially your parents, may be having a difficult time not thinking about your depar-ture. I know it's hard to take when they call you their "baby," but most parents have similar feelings. You barely remember your tod-dler days, but to parents those early years remain forever etched in their memories, and you can imagine that if they can't seem to let go of those memories, it is going to be tough for them to let go of their source—you. And even though you may miss home when you first get to college, your days will be so filled with new things that you proba-bly won't have that much time to be homesick. But your departure will leave a void with your parents that will be much harder for them to fill.

Exactly how they feel will depend somewhat on your birth order. If you're the first one to leave the nest, it's definitely going to be dif-ficult for them. If you're in the middle, they'll have had a taste of what it's like and may not react so badly. If you're the last one to go, leaving behind the so-called "empty nest," then their reaction might be even stronger than for their firstborn.

You have to remember that while your departure signals that you are growing up, to your parents it's also a sign they are growing old. If parents have been too devoted to their children, and have not spent enough time fulfilling their own dreams and aspirations, then after their children leave, they can feel as if they have nothing left in common. It's called the empty nest syndrome, and in my practice I see couples who break up because of it. While you can't take care of your parents' lives, and the empty nest syndrome isn't ever the chil-dren's fault, I bring it up to show you how serious are the emotions your parents feel at a moment like this.

TIPS

- If your parents are giving you a constant stream of advice, ask them to write some of it down. Don't say that it's because they're driving you up the wall, but instead say you're having a hard time remembering it all.

- Reassure your parents that you intend to stay in contact. This will help them feel less like they're being abandoned. If they don't know how to use e-mail, make sure you teach them, as that's a very convenient way of staying in touch.

- If your parents went away to college, make a point of asking them about their experiences. Remembering that they survived will make it easier for them to let go of you.

YOUR SIBLINGS

If you have siblings living at home, they are also going to feel strange. They may act like they're glad you'll be away, even taunting you that they're going to take over your room, but in fact they're going to miss you, even if they don't fully realize how much.

When emotions are running high, that can lead to explosions, even if they don't seem connected to your going away to college. I don't want to set up a self-fulfilling prophecy here and make you think that your entire family is going to be at each other's throats for your last few weeks at home. This is just a gentle warning that in case you notice some frayed nerves, you have to be a little forgiving. Why you, when you're the one under the most tension? The simple answer is that you're reading this book and so I can get this message across to you. I wish I could be at your house to act as referee, but since that's not possible, I'm asking you to substitute for me. And don't be afraid to use my name. If someone starts yelling for no good reason, tell them that Dr. Ruth said it's because everyone is a little on edge because you're going to college and to calm down. They may look at you strangely, but if it gets them to settle down a notch or two, then we've done our job.

YOUR OTHER RELATIVES

Unless your grandparents share your home, they're probably not going to be as involved in this whole process, but they too will be feeling some pangs of regret to see you leave. The relationship between grandparents and grandchildren is a special one, and the more often you saw them, the more they'll miss you. Keep in mind that if they're retired, the times you visited with them meant a lot. Both your parents may work and so can fill up some of the hours they devoted to you in other ways, but your grandparents may not have the same options.

There are plenty of other family members—aunts, uncles, cousins—who will miss having you around. While you may be home for the "holidays," there will undoubtedly be some special times, like birthday parties, that you won't be able to make, and so will be sorely missed.

Is there anything you can do about the reaction of these relatives to your departure? Absolutely. Some young people get very wrapped up in themselves, especially when there is an important event coming up. While that may be a natural tendency, you have to make sure you spend some time with these relatives, if not physically, then at least on the phone. Let them know that you'll be thinking of them and missing them. Then when you do see them during your breaks from school, you won't feel so guilty for having abandoned these family members.

I know that at this point some of you are saying, "Come on, Dr. Ruth, you're supposed to be giving me advice, and so far you've been telling me how I can help everyone around me." I realize that, but the fact that you're going off to college means you're that much closer to being a full-fledged adult, and if you want to be treated like an adult, you have to act like one. Being an adult means taking on responsibilities. A child can go through life without worrying about how other people feel, but an adult can't. So if you want to be thought of as an adult going off on his or her own, then you have to start acting more like one. You'll see that by developing such an attitude before you go away will help you when you're actually in college.

SEPARATING FROM YOUR FRIENDS

While you're going to have a hard time separating from your friends, I have to say that you are part of a new generation for whom this separation is going to be much different from what it ever was before. Almost all college students today have an Internet connection in their dorm room, and that means you are going to be able to stay in contact with your friends much more than college students ever did earlier. And long-distance phone costs have dropped dramatically, which opens another avenue of contact. Such communications are not the same as being together, but if you can share news with each other, the feeling of being separated won't be so great. In fact, if you already spend a lot of time using one of the messengering programs, when your friends are around the corner, then the fact that the distance will be much farther when you're away at school won't even be that apparent.

That said, you won't be able to spend the time with them that you did before, and so you will miss them, and just as you have to learn to break away from your parents, you're also going to have to learn to break away from your friends. If you spend too much time chatting with your old friends, how are you going to make new ones? Sometimes it's best to throw yourself into a situation, the sink-or-swim philosophy, rather than take little bitty steps. I'll get into this more later on, but it's a point I wanted to address here too.

Of course there are friends, and there are close friends. Most people have one or two especially good buddies. You will miss them, that's for certain, but you can also be sure that when you do get back together during school breaks, your friendship will be just as strong as it was before. With more casual friends, it's easy to drift apart, but with someone you're very close to, that's not as likely to happen.

BOYFRIENDS AND GIRLFRIENDS

Of course there's another whole category that I haven't touched upon yet, and that's boyfriends and girlfriends. While these are the terms we use, these people are a lot more than just friends. They are people for whom you have a very close personal attachment, and it can be wrenching to leave them for a day, not to mention an extended period of time.

I have to assume that if you're going to different schools, you've already talked about this situation and decided what was best for you. It probably means that, somewhere deep inside, you expect that this relationship is not going to last. It's not that you're looking to break up, or otherwise you would have done so, but you're realistic enough to know that at age seventeen or eighteen, this relationship is not going to last a lifetime. It also may mean that you actually want to meet new people, and you'll be exposed to many in college. You know that you'll both be changing, and you want to be open to those changes, but you can't be if you're emotionally tied down to someone not sharing those experiences with you.

If both parties share this point of view, then although the separation will be difficult, it won't be impossible. What can make such a break especially awful is when only one member of the couple feels that way. The other person feels betrayed, and even though you're not officially breaking up, it will seem that way. And so it can get very messy emotionally.

There's no simple solution to these situations. The types of attachments that are formed even in the teenage years can be very strong and you will never forget the boyfriend or girlfriend who shared such momentous events as the senior prom, your first kiss, and maybe even your first experience with sexual intercourse. But you can't build a life on memories. You're both about to make some significant changes. While a few teens know before they get to college what careers they intend to pursue, most don't make those decisions until later. You need the freedom to choose whatever paths best suit you, and those decisions can rarely be made as a couple. In fact, even the lover you might have in college might not be the right person with whom to make a lifetime commitment. Realistically speaking, the odds of the two of you sticking together aren't very good.

TIPS

- Try not to dwell on the moment of separation, but spend your last days together having as much fun as possible. That way your memories of this person will be pleasant ones, no matter whether you stay together or not.

- It may be difficult, but try not to make any promises you know you can't keep. It may be tempting to tell the other person that you'll be waiting for them and won't date anyone else, but that's a promise you may later regret.

- Make a pact to give each other some space. If you talk on the phone to each other every night while you're apart, it will be more difficult for you to form attachments at college, even friends of the same sex. College is a growing experience and to do that you need some room to spread out.

But while going off to college may mean a physical breakup, most young people don't officially break up at this point. They promise to keep in daily touch and to see each other the first chance they get, and in all likelihood when the holidays roll around, they won't have formed another attachment and will get back together during their vacation. What they'll probably notice, however, are the changes that each person has gone through. They won't be able to communicate to each other exactly what their college experience has been like. And when they go back to college, they may begin to feel a stronger urge to look for somebody who is at their campus and can share their college years with them. And by the time spring rolls around, those new attachments may have been made.

Again there are no hard and fast rules about all of this. These are just trends, which stem from the separation that has occurred and the personal growth of each person. Since no two couples will follow the exact same pattern, you can only draw certain inferences from the experience of others. And if you do decide to go your separate ways at some point, it doesn't mean that you weren't right for each other before you left for college. It means only that the growth process that has occurred in college has also made you outgrow that old relationship.

Q. My girlfriend and I have been trying to maintain our relationship even though we're at colleges that are hundreds of miles apart. We talk on the phone a lot and send e-mails, but can this relationship survive four years of this?

A. It could, but it's not very likely, and maybe not even worth it. You might stay loyal to each other for four years, missing out on a lot of fun, and then after your college years, still break up. In my opinion, if you really love each other so much that you want to save this relationship, then one, or both of you, should transfer schools. If being together is not such a priority that it's worth making that kind of change, then I would say the relationship isn't worth stringing along either.

TIPS FOR OLDER STUDENTS

Since I do realize that more than half of all students going to college for the first time these days are over the age of twenty-five, the advice I've just given to high school seniors doesn't totally apply. But let me begin by saying that to some extent it is applicable. Let's take a young married couple. One continues to work at whatever job he or she had, and the other begins working toward a college degree. That new student is going to evolve beyond just becoming more knowledgeable. By associating with other college students and faculty, and by applying their education, these students will find that their views will begin changing in many areas. And one of those areas may be toward the spouse. It's not uncommon for one-half of such a couple to work very hard to help pay for the college or graduate school education of the other, and then find that after graduation the person with the new degree also wants a new life. Now in some of these instances the couple may have split up no matter the circumstances, but I do believe that acquiring a higher education does change people, and so it's something that couples in such circumstances must be aware of.

I would suggest that the partner who is not going forward with their education, assuming they don't already have a higher degree of education, should not devote themselves so totally to the other person that they don't have a life of their own. Growth can come in many areas, not necessarily only through book learning. Perhaps that person may want to get involved in a sport or a hobby. They could take classes in painting or cooking. They could join a book club, where the group reads and discusses a book a month. My point is, they shouldn't be standing still while their partner is going through a growth spurt. By joining in the process of bettering themselves, they will increase their chances of keeping their relationship intact.

And for the student, don't be so quick to want to change everything about your old life. You're not a child and so, even though college will change you, these changes should not be so fundamental that you need to dispose of your partner. You will be exposed to many temptations in college, in the form of attractive, bright, single students. But life is full of temptations, and when you make a commitment, you're supposed to have the strength to live up to it. You'll always be meeting new people who may seem more fascinating and attractive than your partner, but if you go through life giving in to these temptations, eventually you'll find yourself old and alone. There are some drawbacks to having a partner, and not having the freedom to date whom you please is one of them, but there are also many pluses. Make sure you don't forget them.

THE ADVICE GIVERS

Returning once again to our younger readers who are about to go off to the campus of their choice, I have to warn you about a change that is going to take place in your parents; suddenly they are all going to think they're Dr. Ruth. Every time you see them, they'll be spouting some new pieces of advice, and it may seem to you that it's all they're thinking about, finding bits of wisdom to pass on to you. And to some degree you'd be right. Most mothers and fathers parent by the seat of their pants. A crisis comes along and they deal with it. Since their children are always around, they take it for granted that when there's a problem, their child can always run to Mom or Dad. As the day of your moving out approaches, it suddenly hits them that they won't be there to do that any more, and some of them panic. They get a bad case of the "what ifs" and have to go running after you to tell you what to do about the last "what if" they thought about.

To the budding college freshman, it can be a little like the boy who cried wolf. The first few tidbits of advice may have been digestible, but after a while you feel like you're drowning in the constant torrent of information being directed your way. While your reaction to the quantity of advice you're receiving may be expected, don't turn a deaf ear to all of it. The twenty or thirty years of experience your parents have has taught them a few things, some of which you'll definitely need to know when you're on your own. Since high schools don't dole out a lot of practical advice, and even if your parents did tell you some of this stuff before, you might not have been listening all that closely until now, so you'd be wise to pay some attention to what they're saying.

It is true that sometimes the only way to learn is through your mistakes, but where you might start to feel a touch of panic is right after you make one of those boo-boos. It's at that moment in time that you'll be desperately trying to remember what Mom and Dad had to say on the subject. Now if you were paying at least some attention, their words of wisdom might come back to you, but if you made a point of ignoring them, you could find yourself improvising at a moment when you'd really rather not. Here's a common place where college students find themselves stuck—the laundry room. Some teens do their own laundry at home, and so they can safely put their headsets on when Mom gives the laundry lesson, but if you've never done the laundry, any mistakes you make might put a severe damper on much of your wardrobe, which could wind up a different size and color when you're finished. So while I'm not telling you to take careful notes each time one of your parents gets up to make a speech, try to let *some* of their advice soak in.

Of course your parents won't be the only ones giving you advice. Many other relatives will chime in from time to time. Be especially attentive to any of them who may be significantly younger than your parents and who attended college in the recent past. Older siblings may also have some advice for you, though how seriously you take it may depend on whether they tend to pull your leg regularly or not. Some older siblings, on sensing any weakness in their younger kin, will immediately go for the jugular, which in this case would be to tell you all sorts of college-related horror stories. You have to be careful not to pay any attention to those.

The one thing about all this advice you're going to get is that there's no way of telling in advance how much of it will be useful and how much of it won't. Your experience in college is going to be unique to you. You'll have different roommates, different professors, a different major, and a different staff playing havoc with the food in your dining hall. But there may be a few gems that you'll be eternally grateful for, so try to be patient and absorb as much as you can.

THE NIGHT BEFORE

People get ready for major events in different ways. Some of you will be fully packed days before it's time to leave. Others will want to avoid the issue and will be packing at the last minute. But whatever your style, the final twenty-four hours will be hectic, even for those of you who stowed all your gear a long time ago because you're the type to worry about little things and you might end up unpacking everything at the last minute just to make sure you didn't forget your pencil sharpener.

On your last night at home, unless your school happens to hold freshmen orientation later than most schools, there's going to be a major conflict. You're going to want to be with your friends, and your family will expect you to hang out with them. I think it's important that you resolve this conflict earlier rather than later. A simple solution might be to plan a nice dinner with your family, and a last blast with your friends that starts later, unless you've got such a long haul the next day that you'll be leaving before dawn. Whatever the solution you arrive at, don't let your last night at home end on a sour note with everyone at each other's throats. And if you have to choose between family and friends, you *must* choose your family. Your parents are really going to miss you, and they have a lot more invested in you than your friends (including the price of your college education) and they deserve the opportunity to give you a proper sendoff.

Of course, some parents won't make that much of a fuss. Maybe they're very busy individuals. Maybe they're afraid to show their emotions and will keep them bottled up. Maybe your relationship in the past few years has been so strained that they can't get over it that easily. I believe those parents are in the minority, but if you're facing a situation where your departure doesn't seem to be causing your parents any discomfort, don't feel bad if this disturbs you. They should be acting like they're going to miss you, and if they're not, for whatever reason, you should be upset at this. There's not much you can really do about it, but you should let it teach you a lesson so that when you have children and they're going off to college for the first time, you make sure you show them how much you care about them.

PARTING IS SUCH SWEET SORROW

Probably a majority of you are going to be driven to college by your parents. In part that's because these days college freshmen take so much stuff with them. In the olden days it was only clothes, but now a computer and music system are just about de rigueur (hey, you're going to college so I expect you to understand phrases like that). A good many will also be bringing a TV, microwave, and refrigerator. (I'm not much for giving practical advice, but I do suggest that you check with your roommate/roommates to make certain you're not trying to stuff four refrigerators in your dorm room.) Some college students need a U-Haul in order to carry all their belongings. It's a little difficult, then, for your parents to drop you at the bus station. But some of you will be flying off to college, and that will limit what you can take (though not necessarily what you can buy when you get there). My point is that most good-byes will take place on campus, rather than at home. The difficulty is that it will be a much more drawn-out affair.

I do think it is good that your parents get to see you safely set up in your room. They may be a bit overbearing as they help you to get settled in, but with all you'll be bringing, those extra hands will come in handy. But whether or not it's good for you, it's definitely good for them. After they've gone, they'll be able to picture where you are situated. They'll undoubtedly be nervous about your well-being, and having that mental image of you in your room will be a definite comfort. Also, if they've met your roommate(s), that might also put them at ease (unless yours happen to be of such a low quality that they can't hide their shortcomings even for a few hours while parents are hanging around).

Speaking of hanging around, you can be sure that your parents won't want to leave. Since college administrators are aware of this tendency, many have an official time when parents must leave. While no one is going to arrest them for staying, it gives the students the opportunity to force them out of the door.

I can guarantee that most moms, and many dads, are going to be teary-eyed, if not in front of you, the moment they start to drive away. They'll want to spare you from seeing them so upset, as they know this is supposed to be a happy moment, but leaving their "baby" at college is a very emotional moment for them. It's not just that they won't be seeing you for a while, but it's the start of a permanent separation between you and them, and it's not a pleasant experience, I can tell you.

TIPS

- Whether or not you feel homesick, make a point of keeping in touch with your parents the first few days. You can tell them up front that you won't always be calling every night, but make a point of doing it in those early days so that they know you're okay.

- Don't forget to make contact with other relatives too. You can call a close aunt or uncle, and then ask them to call your parents to report that you're doing fine.

TIPS

- When you do call home, be prepared to give some details. A string of yeses and noes is not very satisfying to parents.

But since it's also going to be an emotional moment for you, the odds are that you're going to be doing your best to keep that upper lip of yours as stiff as possible. You're definitely not going to want to cry, even if you normally don't worry about such things, in front of your new roommates. And so this parting is going to be somewhat artificial, as both parties try to conceal their emotions. Your parents will recover, though it's going to take some time. And if you busy yourself with setting up your room, talking to your roommates, and doing all the other activities that will abound, you'll have a much easier time getting over it, in the immediate sense. But that doesn't mean you'll be able to shove those emotions aside forever. There's a good chance that you'll get a bout of homesickness at one point or another. For some of you, it's going to hit only a little while after your parents leave. For others, it might not be until you've put your head on your pillow that first night. And some might wait weeks and even months for it to hit them. There's nothing wrong with feeling these emotions. You need to allow emotions to run their course in order to get over them. Trying to seal them inside of you only causes damage. That doesn't mean that each one of you should spend some time bawling your eyes out. Not everybody needs that much release. But if you feel sad at some point, allow that sadness to sweep over you. A little bit of melancholia won't kill you. And after a while it will wear away and you'll be able to enjoy your college years a lot more than if you kept those emotions bottled up forever.

There will be some of you for whom homesickness is going to be a much more serious issue. In fact, some freshmen can't adapt to living away from home at all and wind up dropping out of school or transferring to a school closer to home. Many more have a very hard time adjusting. Sometimes it is pure homesickness; other times it's a bad roommate or some other specific cause that makes it impossible for the student to remain at that particular school.

How do you decide whether your particular feelings of homesickness are so severe that you need to take some action? I may sound like a broken record, but my advice is to seek out professional counseling, which at a college is not that hard to do. The first person you should talk to is your Residence Adviser, or RA. Each floor at a college dorm has an upperclassman or graduate student who acts as a supervisor for the floor. RAs are close to you in age, and since they decided to take a job such as this, they are usually very nice and approachable. Many are majoring in the helping professions and they've probably seen other students go through similar crises and can help you. But even if they are not equipped to get you through, they will definitely know what other types of counseling are available on campus. Every college has a staff of advisers who continually help students with problems like yours and can be of great value. There's no cost, and you won't have to feel like a social outcast because no one ever needs to know why you visited them. So if you're really miserable, don't hesitate to go see one of these counselors.

Q. My roommate doesn't have a life. If she doesn't have class, she just sits on her bed watching TV. She won't tell me what's wrong. I've tried to get her to go out with the rest of us in our suite, but she refuses. It's a drag sharing a tiny room with someone who mopes around all day, but even without the selfish reasons, I'd like to see her break out of her shell. Any suggestions?

A. Since there are many possible reasons for her attitude—she might be homesick, she might miss her boyfriend, she might be clinically depressed—it's difficult for you to help her without knowing exactly what the problem is. Here's one suggestion of what you could do to get her to open up: complain to her about what a lousy day you are having. Maybe she'll be more willing to talk about your problems, and once you break the ice, that might help you discover why she's so morose.

If that doesn't work, don't hesitate to talk to your RA.

Her inactivity is a cry for help, and while she may resist seeking help from you, who she sees is getting along in college, hopefully she will open up to the RA, or some counselor the RA could recommend.

PARENTS' ADVICE

Usually I believe parents are quite capable of helping their children, but for issues of homesickness, they may not be the best place to go. Many parents will tend to overreact, either feeling too sorry for their child and wanting to whisk them back home, a natural tendency since they're missing them so much, or they'll take the opposite stand, and tell you to just suck it in. This reaction might be a result of the high cost of college, as well as a fear that if you do come home, they'll be stuck taking care of you forever. So while some parents are capable of detaching themselves from the situation and giving good advice, others won't be able to do so. That's why I say to seek out a counselor on campus, even if you admit to your parents by phone or in writing how badly you are feeling.

And what if you only have a mild case of the blues? If you're not too far from home, you could just visit the homestead over a weekend. Just seeing that everything is still there, including your room that needs cleaning up and the garbage that needs to be emptied, may be enough to recharge your batteries and get you back on track.

The one thing you shouldn't do is mope around. There are plenty of activities taking place on every college campus. Throwing yourself into as many as possible will force you to stop thinking so much about what you are missing at home. It will also give you the opportunity to meet new people, and if only one of these people turns out to be simpatico, that's all you'll need to feel more positive about being hundreds of miles from home.

Another method of dealing with an unpleasant experience is to put a time limit on it. Tell yourself that if after a few months you are still feeling miserable, you will then apply to transfer to a college that is closer to home, maybe even one to which you could commute. It may turn out that by the end of your first term you'll be having such a great time that you never want to leave, but if you've gone through the application process and been accepted elsewhere, that escape hatch could allow you to finish out the year in a more healthy frame of mind.

Q. While I seem to be adjusting to college life, I'm having a weird problem with my parents. I know that most parents are always calling their kids who go away to school, but mine never do. And when I call them, they never seem to have time to talk. It's not that I feel homesick exactly. It's more like I feel abandoned. What do you suggest I do?

A. First of all, don't panic. It's easy to imagine the worst, that your parents have forgotten all about the moment you left for college, but it's much more likely that they've just hit a very busy period. Or they may have been given some advice that they shouldn't bug you and they're trying to follow it too closely. In fact, maybe you're the one who told them not to worry about you.

I suggest you start calling other people. If you have younger siblings who are still at home, call at a time when you know they'll be around and speak with them. Call your grandparents. If you're close to an aunt or uncle, call them. Don't make a big deal that your parents aren't calling you, but do mention it to each of these. I bet you that word gets back to your parents and you'll see a difference in their pattern of phone calls to you.

YOUR ROOMMATE

From Peoria or Mars

Unless you've handpicked your roommate, and he or she happens to be your twin that you've lived with all your life, roommates don't come with guarantees. Yes, it may increase the odds that you'll get along if you are rooming with a very good friend from high school, but that's not necessarily the case. If you've never lived together, you can't assume you know all this friend's bad habits. They may not even be under his or her control.

Case: Michael

Michael snored, though it had never bothered anyone at home because he slept in his own room. Michael's roommate at college, Jeff, was a few days late in coming as he was a transfer student. It turned out that Jeff was a 6'3" 250-pound Olympic hammer thrower who had attended West Point and brought with him a collection of swords and knives. After his first sleepless night caused by Michael's snoring, Jeff issued an ultimatum: either Michael stopped snoring on his own or Jeff was going to beat the habit out of him. Michael took the threat seriously and for the next few weeks, he made sure he always went to bed after Jeff was asleep. Eventually, however, the two became good friends, and Michael's snoring became a nonissue.

College administrators don't encourage friends to live together. Part of the college experience includes meeting new people from different places, and if you live with a good friend, this hometown team you've formed is going to encourage you to isolate yourself. You'll be able to pick and choose who to be friends with, and maybe miss out on meeting people who are different and yet who have a lot to offer. In this new world we live in, which seems to be getting smaller all the time, you have to look at the entire globe as your potential community. There's no better place to learn to adapt to different cultures than in a college dorm.

If you spend your first few weeks feeling a little lost, you'll be forced to meet other students, some of whom you won't have that much in common with, but whom you otherwise might never come into contact with. College is supposed to broaden you, not encourage you to live in the same shell you've always inhabited. That's why my favorite animal is the turtle because to get around he must stick his neck out, and you should emulate his daring behavior.

Q. John lived across the street from me and he and I have been best buddies since we were three years old. We never considered going to different colleges and always assumed we'd be roommates. In fact all though high school we talked about how much fun we were going to have. We've been rooming together for a month now and I'm ready to pull my hair out. John and I both love music, but when I study, I need peace and quiet, while John always did his homework with the radio blasting. When I ask him to turn it off, he says he can't live without music, but I can't study with it on. What do we do? I can't just switch roommates and dump John? Or can I?

A. As you've already learned, sometimes being friends can be more of a problem than being strangers. If your roommate wasn't your best friend, you probably would have worked out some sort of compromise much more easily, but obviously you can't seem to do that with John.

There's no need for you two to give up your friendship or even switch rooms. You just have to reach a compromise. What I suggest you do is go out and buy your friend a very good set of earphones, maybe even wireless ones, so that he can roam wherever he wants. Don't think about what they cost, because you're trying to save a very important friendship. When you give them to him, ask him very nicely if he wouldn't mind wearing them when you study or you're going to flunk out. If he refuses, then John's not the friend you thought he was. But my guess is that he will use them, and then you can continue rooming together.

Another reason not to room with a good friend is that you'll end up spending a lot of time with your roommate. Even married people take a break from each other, and they're in love with each other. If your roommate is not your best friend, then you can divide your time between being with your friends and being in your room with your roommate. Having some distance between you and your roommate might make it easier to study. Good friends tend to goof around more, and they have a harder time telling the other to be quiet. Also, who are you going to complain to about your roommate if he or she is your best friend?

But after making my best case for having a stranger as a roommate, I have to admit that there are also difficulties in allowing your college's computer make the decision about with whom you're going to share 9 feet by 12 feet, 24 hours a day.

Case: Joanne's Roommates

Joanne had barely met her first roommate before she was told not to use her towels. Joanne asked her why and it turned out her roommate had a case of body lice that she'd caught while having sex outdoors. A few weeks into the term, her roommate called from the hospital to ask Joanne to bring her a few things. When Joanne asked her where to go, she was told the psychiatric ward. Her roommate had tried to kill herself. Joanne quickly managed to get another roommate, who seemed normal at first, but turned out to have such a highly developed sense of privacy that she didn't want to be disturbed in any way, including being spoken to. Joanne finally was able to hand-pick her third roommate, with whom she remained fast friends.

FRIENDS AS ROOMIES

When you ask people for their roommate stories, you discover that there are a lot of weird people who manage to get themselves accepted into some very good colleges. That's a major incentive for friends to become roommates. But I would advise any student who lives with a friend to be aware of what they might be missing. Before the two (or three or four) of you even leave for college, you should sit down and make some rules that will help you not to be too cliquish.

TIPS

- Don't all take the same classes. If you room together and sit next to each other in every class, you'll never meet new people.

- Join separate organizations. Hopefully you do have some separate interests, and if not, then force yourself to develop some.

- Make an effort to invite new people with different interests into your group and, if possible, from as far away from your hometown as you can find.

- Reach out to others. You could throw a party in your room. When your dorm has parties or meetings, don't sit together but spread yourselves around the room.

- Don't always sit together at meal times. And when you are together in the dining hall, make an effort to invite different people to sit at your table.

You may end up going back to live in your hometown and spending the rest of your life there, so use your college years to experience as much of the outside world as possible.

TYPICAL ROOMMATE PROBLEMS

The Neatnik versus the Slob

Since I'm a hoarder, I'm always surrounded by stacks of papers and books. Luckily my late husband was also a pack rat, so we understood each other, though we never seemed to have enough room for all our "stuff." But when two people have opposite habits, it can be a lot more complicated to come up with a solution.

Some people believe that after the wedding, they're going to get their spouse to change. The truth is, that very rarely happens, and there's much less incentive for a roommate to change his or her habits than a spouse. So if you're in one of these situations, you must adopt a realistic attitude and not try to get the other person to switch lifestyles because it's just not going to happen. The only way two people of such opposite temperaments can get along is through compromise.

While no roommate is going to change their entire personality, most people are willing to make limited adjustments, so the trick to creating a workable compromise is finding out what is most important to each party. There's no reason for roommates to go into each other's closets or desks, so it should be easy to put those places off limits, each to be as neat or messy as the person desires. But in places you may share, like a refrigerator or a CD collection, each side has to learn to give. The slob should be willing to throw out contaminated food while the neatnik may have to give up having all the CDs in alphabetical order. Each person should put their desires on the table and negotiate an agreement they can stick to.

This is the ideal way of dealing with these situations, but in reality many students just suffer through their freshman year and then find someone more compatible the next year. Sometimes there is no other choice because one party leaves no room for compromise and just insists on doing things the way he or she feels like it. But most people are willing to at least listen to reason, and learning how to solve this type of problem is an experience that will serve you well for your whole life. You're always going to come into contact with people who do things differently than you do, and you won't always have an out that's only a year away. Fighting is not a good solution for such situations, and neither is running away. Believe me, any negotiating skills that you develop in getting along with your roommate will be useful for the rest of your life.

TIPS

- Don't make every issue a battle. If you can't stand having dirty floors, then clean them yourself and don't put on a fuss afterward. Just be satisfied in knowing that you can safely put your feet down off the bed without stepping into any grape jelly.

- Don't leave any of your belongings in the bathroom. That way you can be sure your toothbrush is relatively germ free.

- Be as nice as you possibly can. Maybe if you help your sloppy roommate with a history assignment or two, he or she will be more willing to add a touch of neatness to that side of the room.

The Borrower versus the Possessive Person

While this twosome is similar to the one above, there is a big difference—no one has the right to "borrow" something without permission. Many college students look at their wardrobe, their music collection, and the food in their fridge as common property, which can confound parents who find their children returning with all sorts of clothes that hadn't been packed when they left. But while it's okay to share if everyone goes along, people do have a right to their personal property and nobody needs to give that up.

If when you lived at home, you were used to borrowing clothes or whatever from a sibling, you might have become conditioned to believe that nobody minds sharing belongings. But a roommate is not a close relative, and if it bothers your roommate, then you have to abide by that.

If you're facing the other side of that coin, and your roommate borrows your things all the time and won't listen to your protests, don't start plotting revenge. Yes, it would be satisfying to see the look on your roommate's face at the sight of his or her bed dangling from the ceiling, but you would be the one who ends up getting into trouble. Just be very firm about saying no. It may take a while, but eventually your message will get through.

TIPS

- Install locks wherever feasible. You shouldn't have to worry every time you leave the room that your stuff is going to be missing when you return.

- Add name tags to your clothes and other forms of ID to the rest of your possessions so that any fights over who owns a particular item can be quickly settled.

- Make a point of sharing. If you go to get some soda, buy some for your roommate. If you buy a new CD, make a cassette copy for your roomie. Let them know that you're not selfish, but that you like to keep your belongings to yourself.

Q. I'm a slob, I admit it. My mom was always on my case at home, and I had to listen, but I figured once I got to college, I could do whatever I wanted. Now I've got a roommate who's as bad as my mom was, and I can't take being constantly reminded to put my things away. I spoke to my RA about changing roommates, but he said he'd have a hard time selling "Pigpen" as a roommate to somebody else. Don't I have any rights?

A. At the orphanage in Switzerland where I grew up, while the boys were taught the traditional subjects, we girls were only given lessons in how to clean. So you can imagine that now that I don't have to, I never want to have to clean anything again. But while I sympathize with your plight, the fact is that by agreeing to go to college, you knew you were going to share a room with someone. If your sloppiness reaches the point where it interferes with your roommate, for example if a sizable amount of the limited floor space you share is taken up by a big pile of your dirty clothes, then I've got to side with your roommate. Obviously your roommate can't force you to make your bed, but let's face it, it's the sloppy person who is much more likely to encroach on the rights of the neat person than the other way around, so I'm afraid that you're the one who's going to have to compromise to a greater degree.

Nudity

If you've always had your own room, and never were on an athletic team, you may not be used to displaying your naked body in public. Nor might you be used to seeing other people, even of the same sex, without their clothes on. Many students about to enter college worry about this particular issue, and for most of them it soon becomes a nonissue. Roommates usually adapt quickly to each other's presence and develop routines that feel comfortable, which may or may not include disrobing in front of each other. The amount of time roommates normally spend changing their clothes is brief, so even if one party feels somewhat uncomfortable, it's not a big deal. But there are always the extremes—the exhibitionists and the very shy—and somehow college computers do find ways of pairing the two.

The fact is, if your roommate likes to spend a lot of time in the buff, without there being any sexual overtones, you really can't do much about it. You could ask them to be more discreet, but they might turn such a request around and ask if it turns you on, placing you in the hot seat. Your best course with such a roommate is probably to just get used to it, or if you find it very offensive, ask for another room.

Really shy people can more easily maintain their modesty, but not always without paying a price of being teased, especially among males. If the cause of this shyness is a shame of your body, then it really ought to be something you learn to overcome. I know that many men worry about the size of their penis, especially when it is in its flaccid state. Others worry that they might get an erection. To the first concern, let me say that if you can get used to letting other men see your penis, you'll have fewer worries when showing it to a female. And as to the second, if you are really worried about this, then it probably won't happen because having something on your mind is a sure way to prevent an erection. Women may worry about the size of their breasts, or about any excess fat they may have. If you have a roommate who likes to criticize you, she's going to find something to say whether you're clothed or unclothed, so you may as well learn to absorb these barbs one way or the other.

TIPS

- If you prize your modesty, you should select living arrangements that include access to a single bathroom where you can lock the door.

- For men who worry that their penis is too small, I suggest that they look at themselves in a full mirror. When you look down at your penis there's an optical effect called foreshortening that takes place, making it look smaller than it appears to other people. Hopefully when you look in the mirror, you'll be pleasantly surprised.

- If you're stuck with an exhibitionist as a roommate, try to make some friends in other rooms and invite them over. You may have an easier time getting him or her to put on some clothes if you're backed with others who share the same view.

For those people whose modesty is based on strong religious beliefs, it might be better to select a college where such lifestyles are better accommodated.

The Masturbator

Maybe it's because of my usual specialty, but I get a lot of college students asking me what to do about having a roommate who masturbates. Some of them do it at night after the lights are off, which is somewhat bothersome, while others just can't seem to keep their hands off their genitals whether the lights are on or off.

Those who masturbate at night are trying to keep some sense of privacy. If the bathrooms are shared by many people, your room offers the only private place to masturbate. If they're doing it under the covers, in the dark, it's not that they're trying to incorporate your presence into this act. If it really bothers you, which is understandable, I suggest you buy some earplugs. That way you can get some sleep and your roommate can have some needed privacy.

As to the other variety, the exhibitionists, don't let them try to talk you into believing that this is normal behavior, because it's not, and they know it, too. Part of the reason they do this in front of you is because exposing themselves is part of the excitement. With such a person you have to be firm. I don't like to exaggerate the use of terms like sexual abuse, but this is a form of it and you do not have to put up with it.

TIPS

- Give your roommate a copy of your class schedule. Say that at these times you will be out of your room and they can do what they please.

- If you find your roommate masturbating, leave the room immediately and stand outside. Every minute or so ask "Are you done yet?" in a loud voice.

- Tell your roommate in no uncertain terms that you will go to an RA if they don't stop exhibiting themselves this way.

If your roommate insists on continuing this behavior when you are around, then don't hesitate about going to the RA. If they're continuing despite your objections, then they're not going to listen to you, and you have to get some help from someone with more authority. If your RA can't stop it, then he or she can go even higher up, and since this type of behavior could get a student thrown out of school, at some point your roommate is going to have to obey or you'll have a new roommate, or better yet, a room to yourself.

When Your Roommate Becomes Two

In the not so distant past, men and women lived in different dorms on a college campus and visitors had to be out by 11 P.M. Today those rules have changed and some students end up staying the night in their boyfriend's or girlfriend's room instead of their own, which means that person's roommate gets a much closer look at this relationship than they might want.

Forcing the roommate to become a voyeur is usually not the problem, though it can be, because the lovers are interested in each other and usually want some privacy when they're having sex. As long as they leave a signal, like a sock placed on a doorknob, the single roommate can avoid being forced to watch and listen. But that doesn't totally solve this type of problem. In the first place, some couples spend a lot of time having sex, which means the other roommate is forced to spend more time than they wish outside of their room. But even when the couple aren't having sex, they are still an intrusion. In the first place, there's the issue of privacy. You expected to share your room with someone of the same sex, not with someone of the opposite sex. And having this couple in the next bed deprives you of the right to some peace and quiet, because obviously two people make more noise than one. Such situations even deprive you of the right to become good friends with your roommate, rather than playing the third wheel.

Case: Nancy

Nancy's roommate, Karen, started dating the quarter-back of the football team. Since he was the campus hero,

Nancy at first was delighted for her friend. Her feelings changed when he practically moved into their room. Since he was such a popular guy, not only did this mean that Nancy had to get used to falling asleep to the sounds of the two of them going at it every night, but there always seemed to be two or three of his friends hanging around earlier in the evening so that Nancy had no privacy whatsoever.

Nancy tried talking to Karen, but she was head over heels in love and wasn't willing to mess up such a good thing to please her roommate. And Karen said that staying in his room, on a floor full of jocks, was out of the question. Nancy's only other option was to go to her RA, who at first gave her a sympathetic ear. But that attitude changed soon enough and Nancy was made to understand that the need for privacy of a mere freshman girl wasn't sufficient reason to upset the quarterback of the football team.

Nancy was stuck between a rock and a hard place, but many students in one of these situations don't want to complain. They sympathize with their roommate's desire to be with their lover, maybe wishing that they were in similar circumstances. Not wanting to be hypocritical, they don't say anything. Their roommate may also be a friend, and nobody wants to be blamed for trying to spoil a friend's love affair. And since few people living in a college dorm have a room to themselves, where exactly are you going to chase these lovebirds, especially as colleges don't usually approve of such arrangements and don't provide any assistance to students of opposite sex who want to pair up and share a room. (This is one instance when gay students may have an advantage.)

But while there may be good reasons to suffer through such an arrangement, there are also plenty of good reasons why you shouldn't have to. Your primary purpose in going to college is to study, and having to share your room with a couple is just not conducive to that process. No matter how fair you want to be, you, or at least your parents, are paying for you to share a room with one other person (of the same sex I might add). This is not a commune that you joined, and you have a right to ask that your roommate be only one person, not a pair. So while giving your roommate some time alone in the room is one thing, allowing your roommate's lover to move in is another.

People are not always rational under such circumstances. Though you have every right to ask that your roommate's friend not spend the night, or even more than a few hours a day in your room, your roommate may take this request the wrong way. You should try to keep the discussion on a rational plane, but if your roommate goes ballistic, that's a risk you have to take.

There's a good chance that even if your roommate does argue with you at the moment you make the request, after he or she has had a chance to calm down a bit, they may realize the error of their ways. They might not want to admit that it is an imposition on you because they so badly want to spend the time with their boyfriend or girlfriend. But no one ever died from being kept apart, and if the relationship lasts long enough, the two lovebirds can eventually get their own apartment off campus.

When you make this complaint, there is of course the risk that your roommate is going to hate you. Suddenly you will become the parent figure they thought they had left behind. Living in a small space with someone who despises you is not easy. But as long as you have other friends, it may still be the better choice. As I said, your main purpose for going to college is to learn, and if sharing your room with a couple is a serious distraction, then you are obliged to put an end to it.

TIPS

- Try to nip this type of situation in the bud. If you allow your roommate to share his or her bed without saying a word for an entire month, then you're going to have a more difficult time convincing them to separate than if you speak up after the second night.

- If you have access to another bed—for example, if you know someone who goes home many weekends—offer the couple a few nights alone, but in exchange let them know that the rest of the time you don't want to share your room with a third person.

TIPS

- Make a point of becoming friendly with your RA. That will make it a bit easier if you have to lodge a complaint somewhere down the line.

Case: James

When James met his roommate, Greg, they quickly became fast friends. The word in the dorm was that these two hunks were going to be the darlings of all the girls, and the guys were looking forward to having a good time together. However, after about two weeks Greg met up with a girl, and after only a brief interlude, moved in with her. The only night he spent with James was on parents weekend. Greg's parents took the two young men out to dinner and James protected his roommate by acting as if they were fast friends, when in fact they barely saw each other.

While it seemed that James had a good deal, with a room all to himself, he felt that he was actually missing out on part of his college experience. He made friends with the guys across the hall, but it was a different relationship and some nights James felt rather lonely.

In truth, Greg, like James, also missed out. Eventually he would marry and have the experience of living with a woman, but he never got to share in the special companionship that two roommates can have. Falling in love is not something that you can totally control, but this story serves as an example of why it might be better not to rush into any very tight relationships in the first few weeks of college so that you leave open the possibility of bonding with lots of different people.

Gay Students

While gay people face certain problems in real life, a college campus can actually be an ideal place to live. Gays can easily congregate, and gay couples will have little difficulty sharing a room.

Where problems can arise is during the freshman year when a heterosexual person is paired with a gay person. If the gay person lets their roommate know of their sexual orientation, or if it comes out after a while, this might make the heterosexual person uncomfortable, who, in turn, can make things uncomfortable for the gay person.

Case: Jed

Jed had been sharing his room with Hugh for about six months when Hugh admitted to Jed that he was gay—and that he was attracted to Jed. Jed was taken aback by this and didn't quite know what to do. He thought of going to his RA, but he didn't quite feel comfortable talking to her about it. She was only a few years older than Jed, and since he always saw her gabbing with the students, he couldn't be sure what he had to say would remain private.

Jed decided to go to the rabbi who was the head of the Hillel organization on campus. He knew that at the very least, whatever he told the rabbi would be confidential. He talked about the situation with the rabbi and at the end felt much better, to the point where he was able to say, "Well at least somebody finds me attractive." Later that night he had a long talk with Hugh, explaining to him that he was flattered but not interested. After that they were able to remain both friends and roommates.

The type of situation Jed found himself in was embarrassing, and I am all for seeking out an adult, rather than a peer adviser, when confronted with a problem that you really don't want to have spread around campus. As Jed found out, once the two roommates have talked about the situation and set the appropriate limits, they can get along just as they would if they didn't have this difference. But occasionally such a mixed relationship does cause problems. Sometimes the heterosexual person feels ill at ease, without any just cause, and sometimes, as happened with Hugh, the gay person develops an attraction to their roommate even though they know that their room-mate doesn't share their sexual orientation.

The key word in dealing with such issues is respect. If both room-mates can maintain their respect for each other, then accommodation is possible. If, on the other hand, one of the two causes a confronta-tion, then outside counseling will definitely be needed.

TIPS

- Try to keep this area of your relationship with your room-mate private. The two of you may come to an accommo-dation, but it may be a fragile one if other people know about it. Also it's not anyone else's job to "out" anyone that doesn't want this information commonly known.

- Make an attempt to find areas of common interest on which to base a friendship. If the gay roommate hangs out only with other gays, it is going to make it more dif-ficult for the straight roommate to adjust, and vice versa. But if you do things together, like going to the movies, then you'll have common topics to talk about.

If the heterosexual roommate is intolerant of the gay roommate, then someone of higher authority must be brought into this picture as soon as possible.

Rating Colleges for Gay Acceptance

While most college administrations attempt to be neutral when it comes to a student's sexual orientation, the student body isn't neces-sarily so.

Because of this, gay students are going to feel more at ease at some colleges than others, and usually the gay population is much higher at those colleges that are more open to gays. Some of the organiza-tions that rate colleges include this information, and if you are gay, I would advise you to use these ratings when making your selection. That way, even if a problem arises with your particular roommate, you can easily make a change without too much turmoil.

Religious Differences

One would hope that people with different religious beliefs would tolerate each other, given that the basis for most religions is the very same God. But since people have been killing each other for centuries over religious conflicts, it shouldn't come as a total surprise that religion can be a factor in disturbing the relationship between college roommates.

That roommates have different religions shouldn't be a problem per se, as long they are tolerant of each other's religious beliefs. That also goes for someone who does not have strong or any religious beliefs. They, too, shouldn't interfere in their roommate's desire to practice a particular religion.

But because college students are making so many decisions for themselves for the first time, religion can become a touchy subject. There are those students who practiced a religion for most of their lives under the close supervision of their parents and they now find themselves questioning these values, particularly in light of the college atmosphere that has them questioning so many beliefs. Many of these students who move away from religion during their college years go back to it once they leave the college environment, but during their stay in college they can become intolerant of those who retain their beliefs. Or if not intolerant, let's say disrespectful.

Perhaps they are trying to test the religious beliefs of others as part of their own search for religion. But whatever the reason, they can make it uncomfortable for someone who outwardly practices a particular religion.

While having debates about politics or literature or most other topics should be part of everyone's college experience, because it is through such discussions that you actually help solidify your own opinions, religion is one topic where such debates can get very personal. The person attacking a religion may look at it as a sport, but the person whose beliefs are being challenged can be badly hurt.

Q. I'm Jewish and my roommate is a Born Again Christian. He thinks it's his duty to convert me to Christianity.

He says if he can't do this, I'll burn in hell and he doesn't want that to happen to me. Other than on a religious level, we get along okay, but he'll bring it up at least once a day and it bothers me. I've asked him to stop, but he won't. What should I do?

A. Here's my suggestion. Tell him you know that he wants to convert you, but rather than going over the same arguments over and over, how about spending five minutes together in silent prayer. During this time he can pray that you will become a Christian, and you can pray about anything you want, even that he'll convert to Judaism if you want. If he refuses, then you may have to go to your RA and apply to change rooms.

While I think it is perfectly proper to ask questions about religions in general, it is rude to question another person's religious beliefs. Unless they bring up their own doubts, you should never try to poke holes in anyone else's religion.

TIPS

- If you find yourself on the defensive about your religion, try not to allow yourself to be dragged into debates. These rarely convince anyone and usually only lead to bad feelings.

- If there is a religious leader of your denomination on campus, go to them with any problems you might encounter. They have the experience and can help you to find ways of handling the problems.

- If someone is trying to convince you to join their religion, and you'd rather not, don't become negative. They can't actually convince you to believe, for faith is rarely something that you find outside yourself, so if you don't look at it as a threat, you'll be less likely to overreact.

Cults

While cults aren't as popular as they once were, you can usually find a few representatives on most college campuses. Because cult leaders know that college students are generally more open to new ideas, they will try to prey on this population.

If you find yourself the target of a cult, and if simply telling the person or persons to leave you alone doesn't work, don't be afraid of going to the college administration. Such cults concern administrators, but if no one complains, there isn't much they can do. They should definitely be able to help protect you, and by going to them, you'll be helping other students who otherwise might fall into their clutches.

Racial and Cultural Differences

I wish I could say that mixing roommates of different races or cultures never caused any strife, but sadly it still does. Too many people refuse to look past appearances in order to discover the person within. And while we are all familiar with the effects of racism when it comes to blacks and whites, it's a fray that's not limited to only this arena.

Case: John

John was born in the United States, but his parents were immigrants from China who arrived in this country penniless. They were industrious and built a decent life for themselves and their children. John's parents had instilled in him this same set of values, so he considered that the main purpose of being in college was to work as hard as he could to get the highest grades of which he was capable. John was in a suite with three white men, who thought that partying and having fun were the essence of college life. Rather than admire John's work habits, they considered his presence a hindrance to their party-party-party lifestyle. After two months had gone by, they wrote John a note, asking him to leave. John took the note to his RA and asked to be transferred to another room. On the one hand he was glad to be going because his roommates had done everything they could to make studying in his room almost impossible, but he was also saddened by the fact that he had made enemies rather than friends of his three roommates.

John's story is, in some sense, one of culture more than race, but I'm not so sure that if he had been white instead of Asian, his three roommates would have acted so rudely. And if John had been white, I'm also not sure that he would have been able to stick to his guns. Instead he might have been more likely to give in and do more partying and less studying.

As someone who has lived in Europe, Israel, and the United States and who travels all over the world, I can tell you that diversity is a wonderful thing. In fact, I am troubled when I see McDonald's and Coke in foreign countries because I would not want to see other cultures disappear under the forces of the American marketing juggernaut. But it's also not so easy to mix cultural differences, as we've seen in the various civil wars that continually pop up around the globe, even among people who appear to have nearly identical cultures, such as the Irish Protestants and Catholics, and the Hutus and the Tutsis in Africa. Yet even slight differences can be enough to set off killing sprees, so it should come as no surprise that blacks and whites still haven't totally integrated in the United States, as is the case for Hispanics, Asians, and even Native Americans.

The forced separation of the races throughout most of America's history has caused different cultures to evolve so that black and white Americans do have more to set them apart than just the color of their skin. There are differences in language and art and music and food, even as both share many similarities of our American culture. And as long as blacks and whites continue to live in separate communities, those differences will continue to exist.

For many individuals, their college years may be the first and only time when they live in such close proximity with people of another race. While college students should look at this as an opportunity to get to know people of the other races better, and many open-minded students do just that, some have problems adjusting. It is understandable, but I also find it sad that on so many college campuses black students congregate in certain dorms or floors or Greek houses. If we are ever going to heal the racial divide that exists, our college campuses should certainly be a good starting place as there is probably no better lesson that American students could learn than how to live together amicably and fairly.

And while I have been concentrating my comments on this subject to blacks and whites, they apply equally to Hispanics and Asians and any other peoples who live in this great country of ours.

TIPS

- The most important piece of advice I can give to any student is to make a concerned effort to come in contact with students of other races and cultures. That doesn't mean your roommate needs to be of another race. There are plenty of opportunities to associate with other students in addition to living with them. For example, if you are in a class where students pair up to study together or work on projects, try to make a point of selecting a partner who does not share your race or culture.

- Don't pretend that apparent differences don't exist. College is a learning environment and you shouldn't be afraid to ask questions. You should certainly be sensitive about your inquiries, nor should you be quick to take offense if someone asks questions about your background. But if everyone puts on an act, then no real communications are ever established, and it is only if the races communicate to each other that they can gain each other's mutual respect.

- Similarly, don't walk on eggshells when around someone of a different race. Being sensitive doesn't require you to be deaf, blind, and dumb. The more normally you act around other races, the more normal will be your relationship.

TIPS

- Don't allow isolated incidents to set the tone in forming your opinions. There are fools of every race and culture. If you encounter one of these, don't let them "bring you down into the hole that they're in," if I may use the words of Bob Dylan. Move on past this incident as quickly as possible, maybe even making a special effort to meet some other individual of the same race that offended you so that the bad taste left in your mouth from that one incident won't linger.

- And if you do have a roommate of another race who is causing you problems, speak to your RA as soon as possible. Bad feelings can quickly escalate into all-out war if they're not quickly contained. If you do not have the skills to negotiate with your roommate because of racial overtones to the issues, let someone else mediate.

ROOMMATES FROM HELL

Case: Bill

In high school, Bill had been a good student with a lot of friends, which is why his parents couldn't understand why he wasn't adapting to college very well. Not only were his grades not up to expectations, but he didn't seem to have many friends and he constantly seemed to be getting sick. His father, a college administrator, was especially worried. They kept asking him if anything was wrong, but he never gave them a direct answer.

It wasn't until the year was over that Bill admitted the problem. His roommate was a drug dealer. Throughout the year there had been a constant flow of people coming into the room, and phone calls at all hours. The worry that the college authorities would find out and implicate Bill had even affected his health.

Bill's father asked him why he had never complained.

Bill explained that to tell the truth would have meant that his roommate would have been arrested, and he wouldn't rat on him because he liked him. He couldn't ask to change rooms without giving a reason, so he just suffered through it.

Many college students would have reacted just the way Bill did. Children learn at an early age that you don't go running to parents or teachers when one of the group is doing something they shouldn't be doing. What's more, the campus drug dealer does have a lot of friends who wouldn't take kindly to the person who had him busted. In Bill's case, it wasn't that he disliked his roommate, and since Bill did occasionally smoke some of the marijuana his roommate offered him, he would have felt like a total hypocrite to go running to the administration. The longer he stayed, he was convinced that he would be blamed for sharing in this illegal activity.

I understand Bill's dilemma, which is why I would never simply say that he should just have gone to the administration, because saying it doesn't make it any easier to do it. It might have been a recourse the first day Bill found out about his roommate's activities, before they became friends, but after some time had passed, I can understand how hard it became to do that. And let's face it, this wasn't entirely Bill's problem. Someone from the college administration—the floor RA, the dorm supervisor, security—should have spotted what was going on. Bill was a student, not an enforcer of laws. But since staying was ruining his first year at college, and literally making him sick, not to mention putting him at risk of arrest, he also shouldn't have stayed.

Bill did have one practical alternative. He could have told his roommate that he didn't want to stay because he was worried about getting arrested. With all those people traipsing through his room to buy drugs, I'm sure his roommate could have found someone willing to share this drug den, probably in exchange for some free drugs, and then it wouldn't have been that hard to convince someone in the administration to switch rooms. It would have taken some courage for Bill to work out such a solution, but not so much that he couldn't have done it.

As you go through life, you will be presented with many instances where it takes some courage, or some ingenuity, to extricate yourself from a difficult situation. The alternative—doing nothing or hoping for a miracle—is not acceptable. As you become an adult and your parents stop being responsible for you, you have to assume those responsibilities. It's not always easy, but as a grown-up, you have no choice.

3

DORM LIFE 101

As the person who shares such close quarters with you, your roommate is a very important part of college life, but there's a lot bigger population surrounding you, and for probably the only time in your life, the vast majority will be about your age and going through the same experiences you are. Even if you come from a family with twelve children who all shared a rather small living space, you won't be prepared for dorm life, as those around you won't be your siblings and Mom and Dad won't be around to act as referees. Sleep-away camp is the closest experience most young people may have had, but with counselors constantly supervising you, and no responsibilities as far as school work is concerned, it's not really comparable either. So the key word that you'll have to incorporate into your lifestyle is "adapt."

What will you have to adapt to? Noise. Late hours. So-so food. Social pressures. Academic pressures. Nudity. Drugs. Alcohol. Constant interruptions. Playful mayhem. In short, exactly what you'd expect from living with a building full of people who are like you in so many ways.

MORNING LARKS VERSUS NIGHT OWLS

Medical science has shown that teenagers need a lot of sleep, but college may not be the best place to get it. Once freed from their parents' rules and regulations about when to go to bed and when to wake up, college students choose to turn night into day. Since even the best of class schedules will have the occasional morning class, and many college students hold down jobs that may require their presence in daylight hours, most college students do not average eight hours of sleep a night. Now some try to make up for this by taking naps during the day, sometimes during those classes and sometimes in their room, or by sleeping till noon or later on the days that they don't have class. If you're the type who has been used to sleeping eight hours straight on most nights, you can literally plan for a rude awakening.

Q. I may not have chosen my roommate as a friend, but she's certainly nice enough and I do like her. The problem is that she has all these morning classes and goes to bed around 11 P.M. That's usually when the dorm starts jumping, and I have no intention of missing out on the fun. But I'm always stuck going to someone else's room because my roommate needs her beauty rest. Since I like the girls in the rooms next to ours, I don't want to move out. Is there a way I can get her to move out?

A. Have you asked her? Many colleges have quiet dorms or floors and it sounds like she might be happier in one of those, so maybe if you asked her, she'd be delighted. Of course, before you do that, check out if there is any room in one of those dorms first.

If that is not an option, then I would talk to her about some compromises. For example, on Friday and Saturday nights, she doesn't have to go to bed so early. Why not ask her to help you sponsor some get-togethers in your room on those nights. She could split the cost of getting some soda and chips, for example. That would allow you to repay those other girls whose rooms you're always in. Definitely let her know that her sleep habits do bother you, and then see what you can work out.

According to resident advisers I spoke with, the issue of living on different schedules is one of the most common problems among roommates. If you've got a schedule that's chock full of early morning classes and your roommate never goes to bed before 4 A.M., then you're going to be sleep-deprived, and that makes it very hard to absorb all this knowledge the college is doling out. And it's not just nighttime sleep that can be affected, because if one roommate wants to take an afternoon nap while the other is watching their favorite soap, the conflict will continue into the daylight hours as well.

This is not only a roommate issue, because it's usually the entire dorm that's making enough noise to wake up the dead. And let's face it, if all your friends are up, you're not going to want to miss out on the action, whatever it is, so to some degree you're going to have to adapt.

TIPS

- If you're planning your class schedule before you actually arrive at college, be sure to leave some mornings free so that you can sleep late. You can only go so many days in a row on four or five hours' rest.

- Pack some earplugs. There will be nights when you're utterly exhausted and will need to conk out before dawn. Remember, sleep deprivation has been used as a form of torture, so don't suffer needlessly.

- Cat naps can be quite refreshing. Even 15 minutes' worth of sleep in between classes can keep you going.

- Don't abuse caffeine, in whatever form. You need to sleep to absorb what you are studying, so staying up all night before an exam will only have a negative impact.

- If you really are having problems staying awake in class, go to see your RA. This is one roommate problem where there is the potential for help. If others in your dorm report having the same problem, then you can switch roommates so that you share quarters with someone who also likes to get to sleep at a reasonable hour.

NOISE AND OTHER DISTRACTIONS

The noise in a college dorm doesn't just keep you awake, it can also be a detriment to studying. While there are always some students who don't think studying is their main purpose for being at college, I'm certain you realize that learning and getting good grades is your prime purpose for being at a place of higher learning. But if you've gotten used to studying in a quiet room, then you're definitely going to have to adapt to studying in college.

Noise all by itself doesn't have to be a problem. In high school you might have accustomed yourself to studying while you had some music playing in the background. But if you did, you set the volume, and there weren't three, four, or five different kinds of music going on all at the same time, as well as TVs blaring, people shouting, and someone sharing your room who has no compunction about talking to you whenever they feel like it. And the worst part is that you'll want to join in those conversations. You'll want to be part of the action when it's all around you.

I'm going to go back to that word again, *adapt,* because that's what you're going to have to do, adapt to the rhythm of college life. Now, each dorm is going to be different, so you have to be aware of what the rhythms of your particular dorm are and work around them. If there is so much commotion going on between the hours of, say, 8 and 10 P.M., then you can't plan on staying in your room and getting any work done. On the other hand, if things start to settle down most nights around 11, then you know that if you have work to do, you can get started then, assuming you won't conk out before you get done. But if the quiet hour is earlier, then that's when you have to study.

TIPS

- Look for quiet areas where you can study and use them when you have a test the next day or reading that has to get done.

- If you need to use the computer in your room to get work done, listen to a quiet CD through headphones. The music will drown out much of the other noise.

Most dorms are pretty quiet in the morning, when the students are either at class or sleeping. Make use of that time, if you can, to get work done that requires a lot of concentration.

If you are going to college with the intention of getting the absolute best grades you can, or if you're on a scholarship that requires a certain average, then you should consider living in a so-called "quiet" dorm. It's not that these dorms are like monasteries, where no one is permitted to speak. Rather, at a certain time, say 10 P.M., all noise is supposed to stop, so the students can get some studying done. Being in such an environment will most definitely help your grade point average, which will help you throughout the rest of your life a lot more than partying, so don't write off such dorms so quickly.

Q. My family had to take out loans in order for me to go to college. My parents told me that as I long as I kept a 3.5 average, they'd pay off the loans, but if I fell below that, the loans would be my responsibility. I live in a suite with five other guys, who are really great, but none of them have to get good grades for financial reasons the way I do, and I don't want to tell them about my arrangement with my parents because I don't want them to feel sorry for me. The problem is that they are sometimes a real distraction, literally forcing me not to study in order to fool around. This is putting a lot of pressure on me, and I don't know how to handle it.

A. You are learning what it feels to have the responsibilities of a grown-up, which while somewhat unpleasant is not a bad lesson to learn. Eventually you may have to decide between your friends and your GPA, but here's a thought that might be a temporary cure. A college is a big place. There are lots of little nooks and crannies where you can sneak away to study and you won't be found. If you absolutely need time to study, get out of your room and go study where you can concentrate. If you require your computer and have to work in your room at times, then you are just going to have to tell your friends your situation. If you could get them to study a bit more, you would actually be doing them quite a favor, so you needn't be so ashamed of your need to hit the books, but rather they need to grow up a little and take their studies more seriously.

ALCOHOL AND CIGARETTES

Some students choose a dorm that is alcohol and drug free. They've made a choice before they get to college that they want to maintain a certain lifestyle and they should be commended for it. If you are not in one of these dorms, you're going to face a certain amount of peer pressure to partake in alcohol and drug usage, whether or not you're sure you want to before getting to college.

People have been using substances to get "high" since time immemorial, so it's not up to me to be critical of anyone who wants to pursue such activities in moderation. In most cases, for college-age students, these activities are illegal: for all students when it comes to drugs, and for all but those over 21 regarding alcohol. Does that illegality have much of an effect? Apparently not, since getting high seems to be a major pastime on college campuses. Many college administrations are clamping down on these activities, in part because of some relatively new federal regulations, the Campus Crime Awareness and Campus Security Act, but also because their use has been abused. It's one thing to have a few drinks, even to get drunk once in a while, but to get so drunk that you pass out cold is just stupid. And to use drugs that can turn you into an addict is even more stupid.

I don't think most college students would overindulge if it weren't for peer pressure. Peer pressure could have gotten you into trouble in high school, but to some degree it was offset by parental authority. But there are no parents in college, and most administrations step in only when things get totally out of hand.

Q. I have a history of alcoholism in my family. Since I don't want to risk becoming an alcoholic myself, I've al-

ways stayed away from alcohol. I'm afraid that if I stay alcohol free in college I'll be a pariah and won't have any
friends. What should I do?

A. Stick to your guns. You won't necessarily wind up an
alcoholic from having a few drinks, but you must learn to
stand up for yourself. While the "party animals" are always
very visible on a campus, if you look around, you'll find
plenty of people who don't like getting drunk. While they
might not be as rowdy as the drinkers, at least you'll all be
able to remember the good times you have and you won't
be waking up with a hangover.

What offsets peer pressure in college is a growing maturity among
the students as they get older. Some students have the maturity to
resist overindulging when they first arrive, while others develop it
along the way. Actually, becoming more mature, that is to say becoming an adult, is one of the reasons you leave home to go away to college. Otherwise it would be a lot cheaper to go to a college near home
and live at home. But there are some college students who feel that
they'll grow up after college and that their four years on campus is
their last chance to "play." Certainly that's a more common attitude
among freshmen, who suddenly find themselves living without adult
supervision and are not yet ready to assume that role themselves.

If one of the main reasons you're going to college is to party, then
you're not going to listen to me and all I can say is "Be careful." But
for those of you who want to have a good time but still continue the
process of turning into an adult, I'll give you some tips.

TIPS

- Be wary of "party animals." They usually don't hide what
  they're into, and if you start hanging around them, you're
  going to have difficulties not going along. When you first
  get to college, you have the opportunity to choose your
  friends, so choose them wisely.

TIPS

- I believe in white lies. If you find yourself in a situation where people are overindulging and you don't want to go off to sulk in your room, make up a medical condition that prevents you from having more than one or two drinks. If you can convince those around you that to you it's life threatening, they'll lay off.

- One of the reasons people drink is because it loosens their inhibitions. If you're not drinking, make sure you don't sit there sulking. If you're as loud and boisterous as the others, they'll have less of a reason to try to force you to imbibe too much. And if you find the sight of a room-ful of drunks obnoxious, then quietly leave.

Case: Caroline

Caroline moved off campus when she was a sophomore, and while her dorm had been smoke free, one of her friends who shared the apartment with her was a chain smoker. The smoke bothered Caroline for the first few months, but then she got used to it, though she never got the desire to take up smoking herself.

Summer came and Caroline went home to her parents, who did not smoke. After a few days, she found herself craving a cigarette. At first she didn't understand it, but then it hit her. Her body had become accustomed to the cigarette smoke from her roommate.

You might think that the danger of secondhand smoke is exaggerated, but Caroline's story illustrates that it is not. Even if you don't smoke yourself, and I of course would urge you not to, try not to live with a smoker because there are dangers even in coming in contact with burning tobacco in that way.

DRUG USE

Drugs are another matter altogether. First of all they're illegal, and yes, while it is illegal to sell liquor to someone underage, you're unlikely to go to jail for being drunk just because you're not 21. But mere possession of drugs can send you to jail for a long time, and ruin any chances of graduating from college.

Drugs are also habit forming. Now I know that so are tobacco, caffeine, and alcohol, but I don't have to tell you all the horror stories there are about people addicted to cocaine or heroin. I'm sure you've been given that message in high school. What's different about you now is that you're older and that should make you wiser. You should be better able to appreciate the long-range consequences of both becoming an addict and going to jail for possession. You're forced to go to high school, but college is voluntary and you should start realizing that you're working for yourself and your future. Putting all that at risk because of peer pressure is really silly. So if you're not already into drugs, don't start while you're in college.

TIPS

- Marijuana is the most common drug found in college, and usually it is in the form of a cigarette that gets passed around. There are many excuses you could make up to avoid taking a "hit" when it is your turn. You could say you have a cold that you don't want to pass around. You could say you suffer from asthma. Or, since nobody is going to be closely watching you, you could just fake inhaling.

Hard drugs, like cocaine and heroin, cost too much for people to force it on you. If there is no pressure on you to use these substances, then it really would be foolish to risk becoming an addict by going along voluntarily.

If someone is really trying to force you to take a particular drug, tell them that you had a close friend who died from drugs and you took an oath at his funeral never to use them.

THE SEXUAL SIDE OF DRUGS AND ALCOHOL

Some people resort to drugs to "enhance" their sex life in some way. This is particularly true of the so-called party drugs like Ecstacy and

GHB. I'm not an expert on drugs, so I won't comment on what the effects of these drugs may or may not be. What I do know is that a great many people end up doing things they later regret because they were high on drugs or alcohol. Any woman who has sex when she's not in full control is open to an unintended pregnancy, and people of both sexes who have sex with strangers stand a much increased risk of getting a potentially deadly sexually transmitted disease.

I realize that scare tactics don't work and that no matter what I say, or your parents or teachers or school administrators, I know there are some of you who are going to use illegal drugs, particularly marijuana, while you are in college. Will most of you who do suffer dire consequences? No. But after you graduate, when you get together with some of your college friends, you'll reminisce about people you knew. And you can be sure that when it comes to one or two names, the news will be that their life is in tatters because of drugs or alcohol. Statistically speaking, the number of people who die from substance abuse is quite high. The U.S. Department of Health reports that alcohol-related deaths total 100,000 annually from all causes, including traffic accidents, liver disease, related violence, and falls. Fatalities from marijuana and other illegal drugs amount to about 10,000 a year. Tobacco-related deaths are the highest of all, at about 450,000 a year, though this number results from long-term use.

TIPS

- Despite everything you've heard or read about college life, do not assume that the administration of your college shuts one eye when it comes to the use of drugs or even alcohol. Some colleges treat their students more like adults and don't watch carefully, while others will take action if they find so much as one beer can in a room. Ask some upperclass students how your school handles these situations and act accordingly.

Case: Steve

Steve grew up in New York City. He chose to attend a small Midwestern college that was located miles from any

city. The nearest grocery store and movie house were
more than ten miles away, and even that town didn't have
much else to offer. Steve felt stifled at this school and so
turned to alcohol and drugs to "get away." Soon he was
spending more time getting high than studying and his
grades started to plummet. Before the end of his second
year, he dropped out.

There are many reasons why people turn to drugs and alcohol, and
the ones at college mimic those of people everywhere. Would Steve
not have used these substances so heavily were he at another school,
or was this just the excuse he gave himself? Steve turned out to be a
responsible adult, so perhaps it really was his situation, but oftentimes young people don't know why they're heavily into substance
abuse, only that they are and they don't know how to get out of the
hole they've dug for themselves.

Every college campus has advisers who can help you on the road
to recovery. I know that many students don't necessarily trust an adviser to keep the information given to them confidential. My assump-
tion would be that what you say to a counselor is confidential because
someone in such a position has been trained to honor that type of
commitment. But if you would like more information on such issues,
and don't want to speak with someone on campus, here are some
phone numbers of organizations that may be of help to you.

- National Clearinghouse for Alcohol and Drug Information
  (800) 729–6686 or (301) 468–2600

- 24-hour National Council on Alcoholism and Drug Dependency
  Hope Line
  (800) NCA-CALL or (800) 622–2255

- Drug Help: A service of the American Council for Drug Education, an affiliate of Phoenix House Foundation
  (800) DRUGHELP or (800) 378-4435

- American Council for Drug Education
  (800) 488-DRUG or (800) 488-3784

FOOD ISSUES

I don't like to quote statistics because if you look at various sources, you'll usually find different numbers for this or that. But whatever the actual percentage of college students who suffer from eating disorders, they are of a sufficient quantity that this issue cannot be ignored.

I am not so concerned about the so-called Freshman 15, except as it relates to alcohol abuse. If a freshman puts on 15 extra pounds from drinking beer alone, then that is a problem. But even if the extra weight comes from a mixture of beer and junk food, or junk food alone, I would urge you to do your best not to fall victim to this rite of passage. In the first place, it shows a lack of maturity—that without Mom constantly looking over your shoulder, you can't keep yourself from gorging on pizza and chips. It also means that you're probably not eating right, as I doubt that you're piling on the broccoli and carrots too. (It's not uncommon for college students to get diseases that come from not eating a proper diet and that are usually found only among the very poor who can't afford to eat the right foods.) Such extra weight may also indicate that you're not getting enough exercise. And, finally, it might start you on a lifetime of food problems, and that's definitely not one of the lessons you want to include in your college education.

While overeating does have potentially serious health consequences, so can dieting, when it goes to the extremes of anorexia and bulimia. These two eating disorders mostly affect young women, but researchers have seen a definite rise of these conditions in young men as well, though the numbers of men with these problems remain far smaller. As I said earlier, I'm not going to quote you any statistics as to how many people are anorexic or bulimic, but I can almost guarantee that you'll meet some in your dorm. My main concern is to keep you from joining their ranks.

In case you're not sure what these terms mean, here are two definitions I took from the Web site of a friend, Dr. Ira Sacker, called Eatingdis.com. I'll tell you a bit more about him later.

Anorexia nervosa is a form of self-starvation leading to a weight loss of over 15 percent of one's body weight. Anorexia is 15 to 1 more common in females and usually starts in adolescence—14 to 16 years of age—but may occur at any age. Complications include cessation of periods, yellowish discoloration of palms and soles, hair loss, heart and kidney failure, and sudden death.

Bulimia nervosa is a primary disorder that gets progressively worse without treatment. It can be accurately diagnosed and treated. If untreated, the bulimic person will feel an increasingly intense compulsion to binge and then purge. Abuse of laxatives and diuretics is common in bulimia. Bulimic people often experience dramatic swelling of the salivary glands, which leads to enlarged cheeks. Teeth darken, and the esophagus can become irritated and in fact burst. Ulcers are common. There may be rupture of the large or small intestine. Each of these effects can kill you.

These disorders stem from psychological problems, so besides being very thin, sufferers often also exhibit depression, irritability, withdrawal, and peculiar behaviors such as compulsive rituals, strange eating habits, and division of foods into "good/safe" and "bad/dangerous" categories. The majority of people who have these disorders began feeling their effects before they got to college. Normally they begin as teenagers, though the age range is growing, so that even girls as young as five or six are being treated for these disorders, which is in part attributable to what is being called second-generation anorexia, so that these youngsters are copying their own mother's behavior. However, the loneliness and anxiety that accompany leaving home can be a trigger for anorexia and bulimia. In addition, if you get close to any students who are anorexic or bulimic, the competitive challenge they offer to be thin may also lead to your joining the ranks of those with an eating disorder, which is why you must be careful. If you feel yourself succumbing to the pull of either of these disorders, you must go for help.

TIPS

- One advantage of college is that there is usually free counseling available, and so if you do realize that you have one of these problems, it should not be difficult to get treatment.

TIPS

- Some students don't want to admit their problem to their friends, in which case they might not want to be seen going for counseling. If that's the case, then they should go to an off-campus clinic rather than avoid getting help altogether.

- Make sure that if you do go for help, you go to the right people, starting with a medical doctor. While effective treatment will usually include the assistance of a nutritionist, there are medical and psychological aspects to these disorders that require you to see a doctor and counselor as well as a nutritionist.

Case: Phil

Phil noted that his roommate, Geoff, ate very little. He seemed happy enough, but Geoff was very skinny, though he'd admitted to Phil that at one time he'd been on the heavy side. A few times Phil brought up the subject of Geoff's eating habits, but Geoff would get very angry when he did, so he dropped the matter because Phil's health wasn't really his responsibility, though it did worry him.

If you notice that your roommate, or another college friend, has an eating disorder, what should you do? Confronting him or her on a one-to-one basis may not be effective. The person is likely to become defensive and not admit to having an eating disorder. Dr. Sacker recommends that you get together with a few friends and then have a discussion with the person. If several people are telling you that you have a problem, it's a little harder to deny it. And while it may be tempting to ignore the problem, these disorders can be fatal, so at the very least you should advise your RA of your concerns.

If you would like to know more about these disorders, you could look up Dr. Sacker's Web site or one of the many others that exist. However, while the Web can be very helpful in providing information, it also presents a danger, as there are now chat rooms for people who have these diseases and are looking for support in maintaining their condition, rather than getting treatment, and where they can learn about new ways to lose weight or vomit.

If you would like to contact Dr. Sacker directly, either for help or for a referral to a doctor in your area, you can call him at (718) 240-6451.

THE MIXING OF THE SEXES

There are some colleges where men and women still live in separate dorms, the way it used to be at every coeducational college. Many schools founded by a religious group are like that, including Notre Dame, a school where I once very much enjoyed giving a lecture. Now there are some people who find living in any communal arrangement difficult, same sex or coed, and I dealt with that in chapter 2. But living with members of the opposite sex can present even greater opportunities for embarrassment, especially when there are communal bathrooms shared by both.

If this is something you're dreading, take heart in the fact that this is not a new experiment but something that has been going on for a long time and that students have not found life threatening. And if you're looking forward to it because you think it means that such living arrangements are sexual in nature, then I'm afraid you're going to be in for a disappointment. While there are some students, of both sexes, who take advantage of these dorms to live out their exhibitionist fantasies, the vast majority manage to accomplish their toiletries without showing any more flesh than they would at a beach, and probably a lot less.

For anyone who does not like the thought of sharing their dorm with members of the opposite sex, almost every college has dorms where you really won't have such problems. Even if there is no dorm inhabited by only one sex, if the sexes are separated by different floors, then the intermingling of the sexes is more likely to occur in class than in the dorm. In theory it may sound sexy that in order to visit a friend you have to walk down a hall filled with members of the opposite sex, but the reality is that it can be somewhat intimidating. And that's the point of mixing sexes within a dormitory. By removing artificial barriers, you can really get to know them as friends, which in this era of co-equality in the workplace is a very important lesson. I would go so far as to say that having colleges make the switch to coed dorms in the 1960s was an important step for the equality of women in every phase of American life.

> **Q.** There was this guy who liked me in high school that used to try to talk to me and sit next to me at lunch, but he was pretty easy to duck. Now I've got one who lives in my dorm, and it's a lot harder to avoid him. He's figured out my schedule and he even seems to know when I'm going to be in our coed bathroom, which makes me very uncomfortable. I've told him that I'm not interested but he still hangs around. How do I get rid of this guy?

> **A.** Some people won't take no for an answer, and even find that any attention, like that no, is better than nothing. So my first piece of advice to you would be to pretend that he does not exist. Try to cut off any sense of contact. If you see him, don't look at him and don't acknowledge him if he approaches you.
>
> If that doesn't work, then you'll have to go see your RA and let him or her know about this situation. Yes, many people have to cope with someone who is interested in them, but when you're living in such close proximity, it does change the situation and if you need help dealing with this, don't hesitate to ask for it.

Although the point of coed dorms may be to help the sexes get to know each other better on a casual basis, the raging hormones of the inhabitants will create some embarrassing moments. Some young men will try to come on too strong, and when that young man lives only a few feet from you, it can make a young woman uncomfortable.

And because of the proximity of all these men, some young women put up a protective barrier that's more formidable than they really feel. And then there are those who misinterpret friendship for affection, and that can cause some embarrassing moments as well. But just because men and women live together within the same four walls does not mean that there will be an end to the awkwardness that exists between single young men and women who are all potential mates. That potential for finding true love gives off a slight electricity that makes a coed dorm an exciting place to live. Living together won't make you all brothers and sisters, and so there'll be some attractions and some rejections. As the French are wont to say, Vive la différence.

TIPS

- Many young men worry about having an erection in an inopportune place, chief among which might be a coed bathroom. Surprising as it may seem, most of the women around you won't be staring at your crotch so you needn't be overly concerned. And the one good thing about a coed bathroom is if you do get an erection, you'll be in close proximity to a cold shower.

- College women can be certain that the men around them will be looking, but how much the men get to see is up to them. While it can be annoying to be under constant scrutiny, it also presents certain opportunities to attract the attention of Mr. Right. My philosophy is rather than look at the glass as half-empty, see it as half-full. So learn to put up with some immature behavior and just keep your eyes open for meeting someone who appeals to you.

If you encounter someone who is trying to take advantage of the mixing of the sexes in an inappropriate way, don't let yourself be intimidated. If you don't think you can handle the situation on your own, go to your RA and make a report.

In really serious situations, for example if you are being stalked, you can obtain a court order of protection. In case you think that's a rarity, I know of one college campus where more than four hundred students have an order of protection out against someone.

If you're somebody who tends to be inhibited around the opposite sex, rather than giving in to those tendencies, try to make such living arrangements a learning and growing experience. While it is true that when some people get old, they look back and regret some of the things they did, there are also a great many people who look back and regret some of the things they didn't do. I am not suggesting that you do anything rash.

For example, I am always telling young people who are virgins not to just throw their virginity away but to wait for the right person. But if the dorm is having a pajama party, you don't have to cover yourself from head to toe. I'm not saying that you should do things that are dangerous, but on the other hand, don't be afraid to take reasonable risks. Remember that turtle who needs to stick his head out sometimes.

DORM ALTERNATIVES

On most college campuses, the administration wants freshmen to live in a dorm. Eventually they'll allow you to move out into private quarters, but as an indoctrination of sorts, colleges insist that you partake in some communal living. I actually think it's a good idea because if you've always lived at home and then were isolated in an apartment off campus, you might find yourself feeling very lonely. But one of the things I learned in doing research for this book is that some campuses have private dorms. These are acceptable to the college administration but may be a cut above what the college offers.

When I lived in Israel, which was still Palestine then, I lived on a kibbutz and so I know that one can make do on very little in terms of creature comforts. But college students these days are faced with a lot more pressures. A college degree has become necessary to get ahead in the world, and many more undergraduates plan to go on to graduate school. So I see nothing wrong with living communally but with a touch of luxury to accentuate it. Jacuzzis, pools, sun decks, concierge service, dry cleaning facilities, and better food can certainly enhance your college experience. In some of these dorms you can even get a massage. Now I'd definitely pay extra for that! And especially for those who don't like the idea of communal bathrooms, these private dorms are all suites, so that you share a bathroom with only your suite mates.

Because private dorms don't require any additional financing on the part of the colleges or the taxpayers, yet allow for an expanded student body, they are becoming more and more popular. Today's college-bound high schoolers have grown up with additional services at home, greater than those only ten years ago. This new consumer has set expectations on a higher plane. Universities and colleges are changing "business as usual" to accommodate this new market. These incoming students grew up with their own bedrooms and had cable or a satellite dish in the den. In the private dorms available today, you can check the dinner menu on Intranet or write a work order from your room. The Ethernet makes your computer faster for research, the dorm housekeeping staff will clean your bathroom regularly, and the "resident life staff" will make sure you are aware of homecoming events.

If your budget allows for a dormitory upgrade, investigate the possibilities and indulge yourself!

WORK LIFE

With college tuitions as high as they are, more and more students are working while they attend classes. A study done by the Department of Education found that half of the nation's college students worked an average of 25 hours a week, while another 30 percent worked full time. On most campuses, a third to half of the students work for the college itself while the rest work off campus. Students who are working 25 hours a week or more certainly have a much different lifestyle than those who don't have to hold down a job. While you can shift the times you study, and even get some choice as to when to schedule your classes, work hours tend to be less flexible. So a student who works might want to belong to this or that organization, but the combination of a class and work schedule may not allow for such extracurricular activities.

> **Q.** I never pictured college as being such a stressful place. Not only do I have to worry about getting good grades, but I also have to worry about paying tuition. I work 30 to 35 hours a week, some for the college filing papers, and I also take orders at the local Burger King. Sometimes I feel like I'm caught in a vise. If you can come up with an answer, you're a miracle worker.

> **A.** My suggestion to you is to slow this whole process down. My guess is that you're trying to fit all this into a traditional four-year program. Maybe that is too much. What would happen if you stretched it out a bit? For example, what if you stay home for a year, so your expenses are low, and work at a full-time job and then go back to school? You wouldn't graduate with your friends, but at least while you are in school, you wouldn't be so stressed out. Or what if you take fewer courses during the academic year and then take courses at a school near your home during the summer? You've got your whole life ahead of you. You don't have a wife and children to feed, so see if there is some way to spread out the load so that it is not so burdensome.

Since I started my work experience in this country as a maid for $1 an hour while I was getting my master's at the Graduate Faculty of the New School for Social Research, I sympathize with every college student who has to work while attending classes. It makes it especially tough when you see others around you who don't have to put in such long hours and can sleep or horse around while you are working. But what I want to tell you is that you must not allow the fact that you work to lessen your college experience.

You can find the time to do more than take classes as long as you don't give up without even trying. It's always better to have a schedule that's a little too full than one that's too empty. So don't be afraid to say yes now and then and join a club, or try out for a part in the school play or whatever, and then figure out a way to cram it all in.

TIPS

- Don't be afraid to let your professors know that you have a job. Most teachers have learned to turn a deaf ear to students with poor excuses for not doing their assignments on time, but that doesn't mean they aren't willing to make exceptions when they know the need is there.

- On the other hand, don't allow your friends to think you're never available because of your job. Make a point of putting aside time so that you can take part in at least some of their activities.

- If you have a choice of jobs, don't let the pay rate be the only deciding factor. Obviously if one teaches you something of value, that should be your first choice. But if you can find a job where you can also crack open a book now and then, it might be better than a job that pays a little more but occupies your attention full time.

- See if you can find a job that will allow you to change your hours. If there are other people doing the exact same thing you are, it's more likely that you could trade, when needed, than if you are the only one responsible for those duties.

YOU AND YOUR RESIDENTIAL ADVISER

It might be natural to look at the RA of your floor, as well as any other residential staff, as replacement of parental authorities and then try to have as little contact with them as possible. That would be a mistake. In the first place, they don't want to be your parents and would prefer to never have to exercise any authority. But if the occasion arises that you do run afoul of them, if you're on good terms, you'll be a lot better off than if they hardly know you.

Case: Jane

Jane was an only child, and her parents catered to her every whim. She had never shared a room with anybody, and the experience of not being in charge was a little overwhelming to her. She was barely communicating with her roommates. She didn't complain, but when her mom found out, she didn't hesitate to get on the phone with Fran, the dorm's RA. Fran went to investigate, and though it was clearly Jane's fault, the rift between roommates seemed too big to heal, so she helped Jane switch rooms. It didn't take very long for Jane to have similar problems with this new roommate.

Fran decided that Jane needed some special attention, so she took her under her wing. They spent long hours talking, and eventually Jane realized that, when living with a roommate, she couldn't always have her way and that she had to learn to compromise. Jane and Fran ended up becoming friends and actually shared a room the next year.

Obviously not every case resembles this one with Jane. Sometimes an RA has to be the bad guy and enforce the rules. Usually it's because the students have not just put their toe over the line, but have gone 100 yards beyond it. But while RAs are not looking for confrontations, they do have the weight of the entire college on their side, so if one of them gets on your case for behavior that you know is against the rules, don't try to give them a hard time. Instead, say you're sorry and try to clean up your act.

TIPS

• RAs are a good source of information about your campus, so make a point of talking to them when you have a chance. You never know what useful information you might learn, and you even might make a friend.

TIPS

- Never hesitate to go to an RA with a problem. You can always tell them that you don't want them to intervene, but they might have a suggestion that will be really useful to you. Also, by reporting a problem early on, if you later do need assistance, you'll have proved to the RA that this is not just a one-time occurrence.

- Try to extend your level of contact with dorm staff to include the resident director and others. They too may one day be of service and certainly can provide you with good information. This is the information age and you can never have too much, so use these valuable resources.

4

ALONE IN A SEA OF 20,000 PEOPLE

Many students heading for college worry that they'll be alone and won't be able to make any friends. For the vast majority that usually turns out not to be the case, but there are those who find themselves alone most of the time. Their roommate may have a girlfriend or boyfriend on campus and so spends all their time with that other person. If they don't manage to make friends in the first few weeks, it can seem as if everyone else has already bonded with other people, leaving them out in the cold.

Why do some people wind up feeling lonely while others have more friends than they can deal with? It might be related to their background. Maybe they've always had difficulties making friends, but if they had the support of their family, they could cope more easily than on a college campus far from home. Or perhaps they never had to make friends. They grew up with a set of children who lived near them and went to the same school, and so they never needed to develop social skills. Another factor might be the type of high school they went to. Students in large schools are forced to learn to make friends, or wind up alone, while students in small schools almost have no choice but to become friends.

If the college you go to is a different type, for example if you're going from a small parochial school to a large state university, the culture shock alone might keep you from meeting people. And then sometimes it's just a quirk of fate. As I said, your roommate turns out not to be there for you and the people you try to meet either are not right for you or reject you for some unknown reason.

Q. I come from a big family. I have three sisters and two brothers. I never lacked for people to play with or hang out with as we all got along and would spend hours playing together. We all had friends at school, but we would also spend a lot of time with just the six of us. Being at college is really the first time that I've been by myself and I feel lost. It's like a part of me has been cut off. My roommate is friendly enough, but she's in the band and spends a lot of time rehearsing. Maybe it's because I never needed to learn how to make friends, but it seems I'm having a hard time and I feel lonely much of the time. What can I do to change that?

A. First of all, you have to define what being lonely means. I think your expectations are set at a very high level. You've gotten used to being constantly surrounded by your family. Probably if you got married and you worked with your husband at home so you were always together, you'd still miss your siblings, even though you couldn't really complain about being lonely.

So maybe instead of using a negative term, lonely, you should say to yourself that you have to adjust to being away from your family. That way, instead of looking to replace all five of your siblings at once, you'll be able to find comfort just being with one other person. If that doesn't work for you, you may have to join a sorority, but since you can't always live in such surroundings, it would probably be a good idea if you started making this adjustment now.

While I admit that it can be devastating to be "alone" when you're far from your family and friends and when everybody around you seems to be having a great time, the good news is that you're in an environment where you can do something positive about your situation. You go to classes that are filled with young people. There are activities organized by the college. There are organizations to join. There are religious institutions you can get involved with. So while it may not be your fault if you find yourself at a certain point without any real friends, it *is* your fault if you don't do something about it.

TIPS

- When it comes to making friends, don't procrastinate. If at 6 P.M. on Friday night you're alone with nothing to do, it's going to be more difficult to correct this situation than if you start working on your Friday night plans on Monday. What I suggest you do is check out your campus paper for upcoming activities. Let's say there's a concert coming up. When you're in class, or in the dorm or in the dining hall, you could casually ask people if they are going, and if you find somebody who says yes, you could ask them if they'd like to go with you.

- Don't think that if you don't have a date you're "alone." College students are dating less and going out more in groups. Since a group is much easier to join, that should be your first aim. If you can't find one, try to form one. You can be sure there are other people in your situation who would love to have company to go to see a movie or hoist a few at a local bar.

While having a best friend is great, don't assume that because someone agrees to accompany you to the football game, they immediately want to be your best friend. Many people scare off potential lovers by coming on too strong, but you can also have the same negative effect on friends. This caution may apply especially to a person who's felt alone for a while and suddenly finds someone who is more friendly. If you try to get too close to them out of desperation, the likely consequence will be that they feel overwhelmed and will then try to stay away from you.

NONTRADITIONAL WAYS OF MAKING FRIENDS

Sometimes the best way to make friends is to put the idea out of your head altogether. Instead of looking for friends, try seeking out ways to use your spare time that will bring you in contact with other people, but for which socialization is not the main purpose. The following are some possibilities.

Giving Back to Society

Recently New York University made a survey of its students, asking what types of activities they wanted more opportunities to partake in. Far and away the number one choice was community service. While students today are focused on their future as wage earners, they are also very interested in giving back to our society in various ways. This is a wonderful trend that I absolutely urge you to share, especially if you are in need of a psychological lift. You may have heard the expression that it is better to give than to receive, but you may not yet have realized how true it is. The satisfaction you can obtain through helping others is really very gratifying. At the same time, you'll be with other people who share in this spirit of volunteerism, some of whom are likely to become friends.

The first thing you should do is to check out what opportunities there are to volunteer at your college. If there is a broad selection, then you probably won't have any difficulties finding an area that interests you. If not, then perhaps you can check out what types of organizations exist in the surrounding community. For example, now that you're living among so many young people, this might be the perfect time to offer your services to some older people. Maybe they'll remind you of your own grandparents. At least the contrast should make the experience more interesting.

TIPS

- Use this opportunity to perform community service as a learning experience. For example, if you live in an area where there are no homeless people, you could volunteer to help the homeless in your college town. Not only will you be doing a good deed, but you'll be gaining knowledge about an issue that affects us all to some degree.

TIPS

- If it's an election year, look into working n some local campaigns. Even if you're registered to vote in your hometown, seeing how government works on a grass-roots level will affect how you view politics and government in general.

- If you start working for one organization and you find it really doesn't appeal to you, don't remain in it out of guilt. It may end up souring you toward volunteerism for the rest of your life, which will certainly not be a benefit to society. But if you do decide to leave one organization, make certain you substitute another as soon as possible.

Religious Life on Campus

Colleges all across the country are reporting an increase in the interest that students have in religion. This awakening spirituality is certainly a positive force and one to be welcomed. If you already belong to a religion, then you should definitely check to see whether your religion is represented and make an effort to attend services. Campus-based religious organizations almost always have a social component to their activities, so by becoming an active member, you will no doubt find yourself making new friends.

If you don't have a strong feeling for one particular religion, use this opportunity to sample what several different religions have to offer. Make sure to go in with an open mind; you never know what you can discover. And by speaking to people who do share a particular faith, you will be given the opportunity not only to learn about a particular religion, but also to meet people you may want to have as friends, even if you don't end up sharing their religious beliefs.

TIPS

- There's a vast difference between a religion and a cult. Cults tend to hide behind certain artifices, like acronyms, so be wary about joining any group that does not openly state what it is about. The number of cults on a college campus tends to wax and wane.

TIPS

- If you have any doubts about a particular group, check it out before getting too deeply involved.

- If you have any particular skills, see if you can put them to use. For example, if you play a musical instrument, there's a good chance you could play at a service. That will multiply your opportunity to make friends, as the other people who play will share one more common interest with you.

Religious leaders can attend to more than your spiritual needs. If you let them know you are lonely, they may be able to help you to make connections. But if you put on a happy face and never tell them anything, they won't assume that they should be trying to alleviate your loneliness.

Working

Whether or not you are in need of employment to pay your expenses, getting a job while you're in college is another way of meeting people. And everyone can always use some extra money, so even if you don't meet anyone you particularly like in your workplace, you haven't entirely wasted your time.

That's actually a point I make to people who are not in college and who are looking to meet people. I tell them to take classes in subjects that interest them so that even if they don't meet anyone during the course, at least they learned something. You already take courses, but if there are activities or clubs that interest you, make sure you join them. Maybe there's a hiking club. Or a ski club. Or maybe you enjoy politics and you could get involved in the student government. Whatever it is, if you like what you are doing, then it can never be a waste of time.

One set of jobs available to students are those provided by the college. An advantage these have is that you'll probably be working alongside other students, who can turn out to be friends. One group of students who do seem to bond well are those that act as tour guides. Perhaps the reason they take on this particular assignment is because they are friendly people by nature, but it certainly can't hurt you to join them.

If you work off campus, you'll be exposed to an entirely different set of people. It will give you an opportunity to become more involved with the town itself, which you should turn into a positive experience. I think it's a little sad when students choose to spend all of their college years glued to their campus rather than exploring the neighborhood they're in. The local town may appear boring, but it's filled with people, and to me, all people are fascinating, so try to get to know some of the local populace. Not only may you make some good friends this way, but they may be able to provide you with information about the surrounding area that you would otherwise not be able to discover for yourself.

To Greek or Not to Greek

To some extent many young people decide whether they're going to join a fraternity or sorority long before they ever go to college. Some schools are known for having a major Greek life and so people who are interested in that will gravitate toward those colleges, while at other schools Greek life is minimum and that's what attracts a different sort of student.

Without a doubt, anyone who joins a fraternity or sorority will not feel alone during their college years. Once accepted into one of these organizations, you will form friendships that last a lifetime. They also give you a chance to live outside of a dorm, but not totally on your own in an off-campus apartment, so they are sort of like a halfway house, with living arrangements that bring you a step closer to being an adult.

> **Q.** I really love being part of a sorority. I've made great friends and we always have a good time. The only problem is that I'm always surrounded by my sorority sisters. We go everywhere together and I feel isolated from the rest of

the students. It's particularly a problem when it comes to meeting guys. You need some one-on-one time to get to know each other, but whenever I'm at a party, I can't seem to get away from my sorority sisters. Any suggestions?

A. You're absolutely right that it can be more difficult meeting guys when you're surrounded by girlfriends. If you're always appearing as a group, none of the guys can focus on you alone. It's great having friends, but sometimes they can suffocate you without meaning to.

You have to make an effort to break away some times. If there are two parties one night, and all your sorority sisters are going to one of them, stay home, saying you have a splitting headache, and then go to the other one by yourself (after a miraculous recovery). Don't feel guilty about doing things by yourself. You won't be living with these girls forever and you need to discover what it's like to operate on your own.

While the ideals of Greek life are quite good, the reality does not necessarily match. Many students join a fraternity or sorority not to become a grown-up, but rather to extend their childhood. These houses become an extension of the tree-house club that kids have always formed, with the additions of drinking and sex and potentially deadly hazing rituals.

Rituals to bond a member into a group go back to primitive tribes. The men, who were hunters, faced life-threatening situations and they had to know that each member of the tribe was brave enough and loyal enough to be trusted. The rituals, which usually included some form of body decorations, also ensured that members of the tribe could identify each other, an important means of communication since they were constantly at war with nearby tribes. Such rituals may date back to caveman days, so they are certainly ingrained into our society, just as is the flight or fight instinct. It's interesting that in this modern day and age these primitive ritualistic instincts flourish most widely among those whom we regard as our intellectual elite, our college students, and not among the lower classes, such as factory workers or coal miners.

Perhaps it is because there is no necessity for this bonding, similar to the real dangers that primitive tribal hunters faced, that the hazing rituals themselves have tended to become more dangerous over the years. It's no longer just about getting drunk, but about drinking so much that it becomes life threatening. And the same is true for the so-called pranks, which can include exposure to the elements, that have proven to be deadly.

As someone who lost her entire family to the Nazis, who prided themselves on being good soldiers who followed orders, I deplore these hazing excesses. It's one thing to want to bond with others, it's quite another to put young people's lives at risk. There is a movement to end these excesses, but sadly the deaths continue to occur.

My advice to anyone who wishes to join a fraternity or sorority is simple. When being interviewed by these organizations, state very plainly that you will not engage in any activities that are dangerous, including consuming large amounts of alcohol. While these hazing rituals remain secret, obviously if the members do engage in these activities, they are not going to want you to join, so such a statement will ensure that you are not put at risk.

Of course there are students who crave exactly those types of hazing rituals because they feel that the Greek organizations that use such extreme tests will also be the ones that will have the wildest parties and where the most fun is to be had. While I believe it is important to have a good time throughout your life, life is not about partying. You attend college to get the best education you can, and that should be your highest priority. If by the time you reach college age you do not understand that, then you're not going to get the most out of college, and that's a pity.

TIPS

- If you're interested in joining a Greek organization, try to find out as much about each one as possible. Don't let yourself be attracted by the houses with the rowdiest reputations. The movie *Animal House* may have been fun to watch, but you have to remember that it was a movie. You don't get to reshoot the scenes of your life if they don't turn out well.

TIPS

- Even if you're part of a Greek organization, don't allow it to become the center of your life at college. Join other organizations and make friends outside of the fraternity or sorority. You're at an age when you need to expand your horizons, not limit them.

While there is a movement against hazing, it still goes on. If you're intent on joining a Greek house that does have hazing rituals, don't allow anyone to put you into a position where you are being physically threatened in some way, especially being asked to drink excessively. Such activities are illegal and you must exercise common sense and learn to say no.

Case: Joe

Joe was a little overweight and had never felt very popular in high school. When he was accepted into a college fraternity, he went all out to be one of the guys. If it was a night to drink shots, then Joe made sure he drank the most. Oftentimes Joe would end up passing out. The other guys would at times abuse him a bit in his condition. They'd strip his clothes off and paint his body different colors. They'd put makeup and a dress on him, lean him up against the front door of a sorority house, ring the bell, and run away.

The next day everybody would have a great time recounting what had happened, and Joe would laugh just as heartily as the rest of them. He took it as a sign of affection, which he was desperately in need of, though in fact he was being abused.

There are some individuals who feel that in order to be accepted, they have to go to extremes. While it's true that everybody in the frat house may laugh about how much Joe drank the night before, being laughed at is not quite the same as being popular. A few years down the road when Joe approaches one of his frat buddies for a job, they're going to remember him as a drinker and wonder whether he's fit to hold a particular position.

A fraternity or sorority, like any organization, has leaders. And to be a leader you need followers, so there are always going to be those members who are allowed into the group but then remain the butt of everybody's jokes. If you ever find yourself in such a situation, don't just continue to take it. My advice would be to go to see a guidance counselor. You won't be breaking any codes of silence about the Greek house because the counselor won't go running to the school authorities unless you report activities that are life threatening. The counselor will only be interested in helping you to gain the needed self-esteem so that you can go through life with your head up instead of allowing people to dump on you.

Hazing Outside of Greek Life

Fraternities and sororities aren't the only places where you might encounter hazing at college. Many sports teams also have hazing rituals. In most colleges these are banned, and the coach might give a speech about it, but that doesn't mean it still won't take place.

Some ribbing of freshman athletes is traditional, but when it crosses the line, that's another story. How can you tell if it has crossed the line? One simple test would be if you could tell the coach about it. If you know he'd object to some activity, particularly if it involves heavy use of alcohol, then you know it's over the line.

Some of this type of behavior can also go on in high school. If you're an athlete, you may have come to expect these rituals, but that doesn't mean you have to put up with them if you're asked to do something dangerous. If you made the team, you're there at the coach's behest, not that of the other players. The coach is not going to condone activities that might injure his players, not to mention break college rules and risk his job. So don't be afraid to stand up for yourself and refuse to do anything that you feel is dangerous.

TIPS

- I realize that going to the head coach and telling him about your teammates' activities isn't the easiest thing in the world to do. First of all, you want to fit in, and then your teammates can make life difficult for you. My advice is to go to an assistant coach. He can act as a go-between, maybe even between you and the other players without needing to inform the coach.

Sports as an Ice Breaker

Although you may not have what it takes to make the varsity team, participating in intramural sports is a great way of making buddies. And in many intramural sports activities, your teammates are just as likely to be of the opposite sex, so these athletic fields can be fruitful grounds for finding romance as well as companionship. No matter who you meet, at least you'll get some exercise.

Even without going so far as joining an organized game, if you have something as minimal as a Frisbee in your closet, you can probably find someone who wouldn't mind tossing it around. For those who really hate the thought of exerting any muscles, you can even make friends while sitting on your butt if you're attending a sporting event. If you're rooting right along with the people on either side of you, the infectious team spirit might make it possible for you to continue the friendship outside the arena.

At northern colleges and universities, very often there are organized ski trips. Since this is my favorite sport, I can't resist putting in a good word for it. First of all, during the bus ride to the slopes you will have the opportunity to talk to people. When you're actually skiing, there's little need to communicate, though again when you're going back up the mountain you'll be seated next to someone with whom you can discuss snow conditions. When you're done, and I recommend stopping before you get too tried because that's when accidents happen, you can go to the lodge, which is an ideal place to meet people.

Sports can be a great icebreaker even in conversations, though it does help to know the lingo. If you're a girl, it's okay to play dumb, as long as you look interested. Guys may look oddly at another guy who is clueless, but that can easily be corrected by spending an hour or so on the Web. There are plenty of sports sites that will explain the rules and give you a quick brushup on the standings of the local teams. Since most of the people you speak to about sports will have a definite opinion, being a good listener is more important than being able to quote statistics.

Student Organizations

On every college campus there are dozens of organizations you can take part in. You can join a group like Amnesty International and save the world, or an environmental group and save the whales, or probably even a financial club and learn how to save your own money. You don't need a book like this one to list the types of organizations; I'm sure all you have to do is go on line and each organization will be listed with where they meet and at what times. You can join an organization that interests you, or maybe one in which you have no interest but would like to learn more about.

Now some of you may be saying, "But I'm not a joiner." While I admire rugged individuality, if you remember the title of this chapter, one of the reasons I'm suggesting that you join an organization is to meet new people and possibly make new friends. Even if you like your roommate or roommates, that doesn't mean you are or ever will be best friends, so it is important to meet other people. Also, these experiences will broaden you as a person, which is one of the reasons you're going to college in the first place.

Q. I suppose I'm what you call an introvert. If I've got a good book, I don't really mind being alone. But by sitting in my room all the time, I know that I'm missing out on what college is supposed to be all about. Even though I'd like to join some clubs, I don't feel comfortable meeting new people. I'd probably do okay once I got started, but it's that initial move that scares me, and so I end up playing it "safe" and staying by myself. I can't change my personality, or can I?

A. Don't look at it as having to change your personality. Since you wrote to me, you obviously realize that you have a problem and that you would like to have more friends. So that's a part of your personality also. What you have to do is learn to emphasize the "friendly" you over the "solitary" you.

One way to do that is to make yourself useful. I don't know what special skills you actually have, but let's say you play the piano. There's a good chance that one of the religious groups needs someone to play at their services to back up the chorus. You wouldn't be asking them a favor, you'd be doing them a favor by playing. There'd be rehearsals, after which you'd get to talk to the other people. And that's how you make friends. So, examine the various activities on campus, see where you might fit in, and then offer your services. That should get you on your way.

I'm not suggesting that you just join an organization to sit there like a lump. To get the most out of being a member, you should try to become a leader. Get fully involved, find an area of particular interest, and invest some of yourself in a project. You will be rewarded for your efforts.

TIPS

- Don't put all your eggs in one basket. Some student organizations are vibrant and really fun to be a part of, while others are moribund. It's not usually the subject matter that sets the tone but the people who are involved. If you only sit in on a meeting of one organization, and you accidentally chose one that lacks a soul, it might turn you off student organizations altogether. But if you go to several, the odds will be that you'll find one worth your time.

- Don't be afraid to volunteer your time or your skills. There's an expression that says if you need something done, ask a busy person. People who involve themselves in many activities find the time to do so much because they're enjoying themselves at all or at least at most of them.

But if you're bored, you can waste half the day just sitting around complaining, and then you don't have enough time to do those things that are really fun. Even if you don't actually join any organizations, many of them hold functions that are open to everyone on campus. Look in the campus newspaper and see what's scheduled and drag yourself to a few. Maybe if you can meet some of the people involved and see what they're up to firsthand, you'll be lured into making a connection or two.

Here's a specific suggestion about what to join. Looking at some lists of what colleges have to offer, I saw that some give a course in ballroom dancing. Now if you say you have two left feet, then you've proved my argument and such a group would be especially important to you. During the course of your lifetime you are going to attend many functions—weddings, charity fund-raisers, etc.—where people are going to dance. Why should you have to sit glued to your chair while everyone else twirls around the dance floor? The time to learn is when you are young, surrounded by other young people, so that it's all right if you make a fool of yourself the first few times. And since I'm always interested in how you can get the sexes together, trust me when I tell you there's no better way to get acquainted with someone of the opposite sex than to be waltzing in each other's arms.

HELPING OTHERS

Maybe being friendless is not your problem. Maybe you've seen some other people at school who look like they need a friend. You could ignore them, saying to yourself that there must be something wrong with them if they don't have any friends, or you could be more generous with your time and see if you can help them out.

I recognize the risk of doing that. This other person may latch on to you, and you might not enjoy their company. Then you're suddenly stuck with a friend you don't want. Because of that you have to be a little careful. Maybe instead of befriending someone who lives a few doors down from you, and who would be hard to duck if they turned out to be a problem, make contact with someone in class or at the cafeteria who seems to be lonely. They may reject your offer of friendship, but if you've got plenty of friends, that shouldn't bother you. But if you can help them out, not only will they feel better, you'll get a good feeling too.

TIPS

- One way of minimizing the risk that you'll be suffocated by this new friend is to make it a group project. If you can convince several of your friends to do this together, then no one person will get "saddled" with having to take care of this person.

If this person is constantly asking you to get together, and you don't want to hurt their feelings, make specific dates as far in advance as possible. If you agree to go with them to see the team play basketball ten days from now, that will make it less likely that the other person will keep bugging you in between.

Another "mitzvah" is to match people together. Even if you don't want to be best buddies with this person, maybe you can help them to get together with somebody else. I'm not necessarily saying it has to be someone of the opposite sex. If you can just get them to be friends with someone, of either sex, then you'll have done a good deed, and you won't necessarily have to spend that much time with them.

Foreign Students

One group of students who frequently do need help are foreign students. They may have a language problem, and their cultural differences may make it more difficult for them to integrate themselves into college life. Because they can also teach you a great deal about the world, making friends with them might be well worth the effort.

Foreign students often have another need. During holidays, when the campus is closed, they may have nowhere to go. They may not be able to afford to return to their homeland for a few weeks, and yet they may not be allowed to remain in the dorm, which may be closed so that the college can save some money on heating bills. Inviting a foreign student to your home for the holidays would be, as we of the Jewish faith say, a mitzvah, a good deed.

You might be repaid many times over for this. Foreign students may be quite curious about how an American family lives, so they'll want to interact with your family. The conversations that all of you have may be fascinating and they can teach you a lot about the world. If you host such a foreign student in your home, you can almost be guaranteed that they would do the same for you if you were to visit their country. Not only might that make such a trip affordable, but you can learn so much more about a culture by living in a family's home than you can staying at a hotel and eating only at restaurants.

DEPRESSION

I've offered you many possible ways of finding friends, but if you find yourself feeling so blue that you can't get motivated to try any of these avenues, then you might be depressed. One of the signs of being depressed is lethargy. If it becomes bad enough, not only will you not try to meet people, but you may start neglecting your school-work and even stop going to classes.

When you lived at home with your parents, they would be on the lookout for indications that something was amiss with their child, but in college there might be nobody who pays attention to signs of trouble.

TIPS

- If you ever notice someone who seems to be falling by the wayside, be sure to alert your RA. That includes someone who looks depressed, isn't eating, is drinking too much or heavily into drugs, or is skipping most of their classes. Making sure that students are mentally and physically healthy is part of the RA's job, so don't hesitate to pass on your observations. You can ask that they not report where they got their information, and they will protect you as a source, but their intervention may be necessary and they can't possibly check closely on every student so as to always spot signs of trouble.

What should you do if you feel that you're on a sinking ship? Go for help. You might start with your RA, but if you don't feel comfortable with him or her (and I admit their sex might play a role in whether you want to talk to them), then there is a guidance office of some sort at every college where experts are available.

Case: Dr. Ruth

When I was putting together my autobiography, I worked with a very good writer, with whom I've written other books and who remains a friend. But when it came time to write about the last day I saw my parents and grandparents, I just couldn't bring myself to cover that material with him. I knew it would be very painful and I couldn't cry in front of him. I found a psychologist who had some experience working with survivors of the Holocaust, and we kept a tape recorder running as we went over that part of my life. I was sad but I also felt a lot better afterward, because he didn't just help me to remember, he also assisted in my viewing those times more objectively.

The reason I've included myself as a case history here is to show you that I don't just talk. I practice what I preach. I knew I needed professional help and I went out and found someone. If you find yourself over your head in some area, don't try to tough it out alone or you could get into serious trouble. There are professionals out there who are trained in helping people with your problem, whatever it is, and you'll feel a lot better after you've seen them. Professional counseling is one of the services that colleges offer, and while I hope you don't ever require them, please don't hesitate to use them if the need arises.

5

YOUR FRIENDLY FACULTY AND ADMINISTRATORS

While the students at a college or university change every year, with additional population fluxes resulting from the ins and outs of transfer students, there is a community that is more deeply seated—the faculty and administrators. Some of these stay on for decades and become an integral part of the school, ultimately having their names carved into the facade of a building. While the vast majority of faculty members are not that entrenched, most do stay for more than four years and so they offer some stability to these institutions of higher learning where the students rotate in and out on a regular basis.

You'll definitely have some contact with the faculty members in the classrooms, but unless the class is very small, it's not the ideal place to form a relationship, though it is an important spot for starting the process. Studies have shown that students who sit in the front of the class, a vantage point they use to help them concentrate and to participate, do better than students who try to blend in with the scenery in the back rows. I don't think anyone needed to do that study because in my experience the better students always choose to sit in front if seating arrangements are not alphabetical, and so this process occurs as a result of self-selection, not natural selection. But let's say that you would normally not sit in front, but could do so. I suggest you do exactly that. Not only do I believe your grades will improve, but your professors will have an easier time recognizing you. That's an important first step in the process of getting to know one another.

Most faculty members have office hours posted, during which times students are encouraged to either make an appointment or just drop in to talk. Usually these discussions are linked to class work, but that doesn't have to be the case. For example, if you are taking a political science course and there's a story in the news that you would like to discuss with your professor, I'm sure they would be delighted to see you take such an interest in their chosen field. And the more contact you have with your professors, the more likely they are to recognize the quality of your work. Knowing what you are capable of will encourage some of them to put pressure on you to work even harder, and that's a good thing. Any motivational factors that get you working harder will help you in the long run. On the other hand, having a relationship with a professor, as opposed to being just one more face in the crowd, may get that professor to cut you some slack if you need it. If you complain about having a cold, for example, they may tell you to skip doing a particular assignment, knowing that you normally do your assignments diligently.

Q. I'm a marketing major and my professor of marketing worked at an advertising agency for twenty years before he left the business two years ago to teach. I'm sure he still knows lots of people in the industry and might be able to make introductions, but he's very hard to approach. I've gone to his office to ask a question, and he's been very abrupt each time. Do you have any ideas how I could get him to be a little friendlier toward me?

A. You may not be the only one who's tried to get close to him because they thought he could help them get a job. He may sense your motivation and, because of it, be keeping you and these other students at a distance. See if you can't come up with a way to make contact that doesn't appear to be too phony. After all, he was in marketing so his antennae are probably very sensitive when it comes to detecting when someone is trying to sell him a load of you-know-what.

Here's one possible way to approach him. Let's say that the events being put on at your dorm have not been well attended and you wanted advice on how to increase student participation. It would be appropriate to ask his aid. But don't do it in a way that makes it seem like you are the one trying to make contact. When you go to see him, take along some other students from your dorm who are not marketing majors, and let one of them take the lead. This may make him less suspicious.

Some professors are standoffish, which doesn't mean that you can't get to know them better, only that it will be more difficult. Sometimes these turn out to be the best ones to get close to, but it may take some extra effort on your part to break the ice. On the other hand, there are professors who are going to be very accessible. If they say they're in their office at certain hours and would love to have you come by, even just to chat, they mean it. And you should take advantage of these opportunities, no matter how busy your schedule.

Professors are more than simply experts in their field. If they've been on the faculty for a number of years, they know about many of the ins and outs of campus life that could be very useful to you. For example, they may know which professors are the best teachers. They may be able to give you guidance on which major is right for you. They may be able to get you into a class that is already closed. And they may be familiar with which are the best restaurants in town.

At many smaller colleges, the professors make an effort to invite their students to lunch or dinner so they can get to know them better. That's less likely to happen when there are 20,000 students on campus, but even some large state universities have programs that foster such mixing of faculty and students. SUNY Binghamton, for example, gives its faculty members a budget to buy students their lunch or dinner in exchange for sitting down with them to break bread. But even if you're at a larger university and there is no program to encourage such mixing, there's nothing to prevent you from making the effort to approach your professors and getting to know them.

TIPS

- Don't wait until the end of a semester to make an appointment to see a professor. At that time of the year there will be many more students trying to get their professor's attention, and rather than having a relaxed conversation, you'll feel rushed and won't have an opportunity to establish much rapport.

- If your schedule of classes and outside activities makes it impossible for you to see a particular professor during office hours, don't be afraid to ask for a separate appointment. Most professors won't mind scheduling an appointment for you. Just make sure that you're on time if they're going to their office to meet you.

- While in-person meetings are by far the best, once you are sure a professor knows who you are, you can also use other types of communication, particularly e-mail, to keep in contact. Don't abuse this form of communication by sending copies of every e-mail you cc to all your friends. But if you have a question about an upcoming assignment, or whatever, go ahead and ask your question, unless, of course, the professor asks that you not send questions via e-mail.

SEXUAL HARASSMENT

I suppose I should touch on the issue of sexual harassment at this point. I don't really expect a professor to take advantage of a student who approaches him or her, but it does happen. For the most part, it's voluntary on both sides, and sometimes these relationships even work out over the long haul. I have two very close friends who are married and have been together for more than twenty years, and she was his student. But professors are in a position of authority, which means that in general they ought to shy away from getting too close to their students because they can, even unwittingly, exert pressure.

Now if the professor is the one to make the first move, you just have to be very firm about saying no. Students can look up to a professor and think of him, or her, as being very sexy just because of the position they hold. That's a mistake you should not make. While it may be okay to fantasize what it would be like to have an affair with a particular teacher, to allow a relationship to develop will only get you into trouble. Be especially cautious about flirting, because what can start out as innocent play can get out of hand. The professor may try to take advantage of the opening you offer, and with their age and experience, and by using flattery and perhaps a little alcohol, get the student to go further than they otherwise would. So my advice to you, whichever sex you are, is not to flirt with your professors. You can be friendly, but at your age I'm sure you know the difference between flirting and just being pleasant.

Occasionally you may have a professor who gets heavy-handed, demanding sexual favors in return for grades. They count on a student being too afraid to report these demands. They may boast that they're good friends with the dean or members of the board and that no one would ever believe a student's word over their statements. *Do not listen to such nonsense.* If a student reports inappropriate activity, the administration will take it very seriously. It may be embarrassing, but if this has happened to you, you can be sure that this isn't the first time this teacher has used this tactic. So you are not only standing up for yourself, but for all the other students who come into contact with this "educator."

TIPS

- Professors rarely invite students out on a one-on-one basis. It's much more common for professors to invite a group of students to their home. If you are invited out by a professor by yourself, be somewhat cautious and make sure your roommates know where you are going.

- If a professor, or anyone, does anything inappropriate, don't hesitate to leave the room immediately. Waiting around will only encourage the harasser. By leaving quickly you take yourself out of danger. Don't allow one incident to grow into something more complicated that will be harder to deal with later.

TIPS

- If something occurs that needs to be reported, don't delay in going to the proper authorities. Sitting on information of this sort will make it seem less believable, to others as well as to yourself. I'm not suggesting that you overact to a comment with sexual overtones, for example, but if whatever happens clearly falls into the realm of sexual harassment, don't keep this information to yourself.

There have been students who have used an administration's vigor at prosecuting faculty members who sexually harass students to falsely accuse a teacher, in revenge for some perceived insult or bad grade, or they have utilized the threat of doing so in order to get a better grade. Apart from being unethical and illegal, students who engage in this type of behavior are also hurting themselves. Grades that are obtained without doing the necessary work don't teach you anything.

TEACHING ASSISTANTS

Not every person who stands in front of a classroom will be a full professor or even an assistant professor. In many universities, which means there are one or more graduate schools in addition to undergraduate colleges affiliated with it, the graduate students are paid to teach certain classes. (In some cases, upper-class undergraduates also lead classes.) These classes are usually supplementary to a lecture class given by a professor and so are smaller. And since teaching assistants tend to be young, and thus closer in age to the members of the class, a camaraderie can develop more easily between you and a TA than with a professor.

While TAs don't have very much clout within a university, they can be an important source of information. I would encourage you to foster these friendships. Because they are less threatening than a full professor, you may feel more at ease asking them what might appear to be a "stupid" question, though there is no such thing as that because if you don't understand something, it's likely that others in the class are in the same boat. And the friendlier you are with a TA, the more you'll be able to use them to ask questions and to act as sounding boards.

TIPS

- One danger with TAs is that the class as a whole can get too friendly with them, and instead of teaching you, a TA may simply lead discussions, which, while interesting, won't help you cover the needed material. If that happens, make a point of letting the TA know you need more instruction and less conversation.

FACULTY ADVISER

There will be a time when you are going to have to meet with a college official, your faculty adviser. You will probably not be assigned an adviser until you've chosen your major, yet it can be difficult to make that choice without getting some advice. So if you're having a hard time choosing a major, go to the various departments that you are considering and ask to speak with someone. It doesn't have to be a teacher but could be an administrator. They know as much about each field, and maybe even more about requirements (i.e., what classes need to be taken before another, and how many courses are needed to fulfill a major) than the professors.

Case: Peter

Peter spent his junior year studying in France. The college he attended offered both undergraduate and graduate courses at its Paris campus. Peter took one of the graduate courses, but because the point system was different for the graduate course, he came home to discover that he didn't have enough credits to graduate. When he returned to college, he went to the French Department and told them of his predicament. At first they were going to wash their hands of the problem, but Peter approached his faculty adviser, who helped him work with the department to devise a plan that created a special course for him, for which he wouldn't have to do any work, but which gave him the credits he had "lost" by taking the graduate course.

You can't predict when you're going to need a friend on the inside of a large institution, but the odds are that at some point in your four years you're going to run into a snag that will require special handling. There are horror stories out there of people who had to take one or more classes all over again because of some administrative snafu. They may not all be avoidable, but many can be adjudicated in your favor if you have made some friends in high places. If you are only a face in the crowd, then it's much less likely that any rules will get bent in your favor. Your faculty adviser can help to guide you through the maze of red tape that can exist in a big institution, but how much effort they will be willing to devote to your particular case will depend on your relationship with them. If the only time you go to see them is when you have a problem, they're not going to have the same favorable outlook of you that they would have if you'd visited with them before, asked their opinion, and then followed through on their suggestions. That's just human nature, and you'd act the same way if you were in their position. That's why I'm telling you to make the earliest appointment possible.

TIPS

- You rarely get to pick your adviser, but that doesn't necessarily mean you are stuck with the one assigned to you. If you find that your adviser isn't helpful, and you've tried your best to connect, then don't hesitate to go higher up and ask to get a new adviser.

TIPS

- Some young people think they know it all and don't need anyone's advice. Perhaps you can get through your four years of college making all your own decisions, but since you have to meet with an adviser occasionally, don't go in with a chip on your shoulder. A bad attitude may come back to haunt you.

- Many college students end up changing their major, which might mean changing advisers as well. If that happens to you, don't cut off your old adviser completely, unless you happen to despise him or her. By maintaining contact, you'll have one more friend in the community, and you can never have too many of those.

FACULTY TROUBLE

Most people who teach in a college or university are well trained, enjoy what they do, and are relatively good at communicating the material they have to cover. But no matter what school you attend, you will encounter some members of the faculty whom you cannot tolerate or who are just plain bad teachers.

If the course they teach is a required one, there may be nothing to do but suffer through it. That may require doing extra work on your part in order to make sure that you get a good grasp of the subject and a good grade. If the course falls within your major, be very careful about how you handle the situation. A bad teacher can lead to below average grades, and the grades you get in your major will be important if you want to apply to graduate school. If you believe that a particular teacher is going to bring your GPA down significantly, think seriously about dropping that class. It may mean taking another class during the summer or having a very full semester at another time, but these are issues you have to weigh carefully. While the easiest path may be to just tough it out, be aware that there may be negative consequences down the road.

TIPS

- Sometimes it's better to sign up for more classes than you intend to take so that if you get one instructor who is just terrible, you can drop that class without having to drastically rearrange your schedule. Of course, if you end up loving each and every course, then you're going to have either a tough choice to make or a very busy semester.

- Many colleges have a system where teachers are rated. The results may be either published in a booklet form or posted on the Web. Check to see whether your school has such a system. If so, be diligent about checking to make sure that you don't accidentally select a class taught by a teacher with a low rating.

PICKY TEACHERS

There are faculty members who, while not bad teachers, can be very difficult. They insist on doing things their way and they will penalize you if you decide to ignore their guidelines. Being a stickler for the rules is not my way of teaching, but students can get sloppy and keeping papers and tests uniform can make it easier for the teacher. My advice to you, if you have this sort of teacher, is not to fight those rules. As they say, go with the flow. Some of these teachers appear to make it difficult to get a good grade, but if you just do the work in the manner they ask, they sometimes don't dwell on the quality of the work handed in, which makes it somewhat easier to get a good grade. On the other hand, if you try to fight them, then they can come down hard on you, no matter how good the quality of your work.

TIPS

- Always pay close attention to what a professor says on the first day of class. If it appears that whatever rules are laid down will be strictly enforced, then copy them down carefully and make an effort to follow through.

TIPS

- Sticklers for rules often set a pattern they follow year after year. If you can find a student who has already taken this particular course, you may be able to get some tips on how to get a good grade or avoid a bad grade. Such advice could prove invaluable, so ask around.

- If this type of instructor makes you very frustrated, don't give up and start skipping classes and assignments. Usually that will only make the situation worse. I would advise you to put in the best effort you can and immediately after class go for a jog or some other form of physical workout to relieve your frustrations.

SELECTING CLASSES

The biggest difference between high school and college is that you get to choose the courses you are going to take. Some people looking at the list of hundreds of classes from which to choose can't make up their mind because there are so many they would like to take. Others have problems because they are overwhelmed by the selection. And then there are those who put in a special effort to develop a schedule that will mean the least amount of work for them.

One lesson you will learn in college is that the selection is not quite as broad as it appears to be. First of all, there are the core courses. Each college has a different name for this group of courses that every student must take, but the basic philosophy of exposing students to different academic disciplines is the same. You can select among them, but usually the selection ends up not being that broad. Also, the courses listed are for the entire year, but some classes are only given during the fall or the spring. And many other courses have requirements, such as that you can't take an advanced course until you've taken the more basic one. So, very often, the only advanced courses you will take will be those in your major.

What all this boils down to is that the list of classes that appeared so vast when you first looked at it will quickly shrink before your very eyes. It is important to realize this early on because the narrowing process of which courses are open to you and which are not begins during your very first semester. It's sort of like the branches of a tree. Once you climb out onto one limb, it becomes very difficult to take any courses on any of the others.

What can you do if you have several interests you would like to pursue? Some people have double majors, while others choose to minor in a second subject. When you choose to have two intense areas of study, you do cut yourself off from the possibility of taking many other classes, but usually two such areas fulfill the intellectual needs of most students.

TIPS

- When you're selecting your classes, try to look ahead, even a few years ahead. If there's a course you really want to take and there are several requirements, you have to make sure you take those so that you can eventually take the course you want.

- Here's another example of thinking ahead. Let's say you decide to fulfill your language requirement by taking Spanish. Then you decide you want to spend a semester studying abroad, but the only program your school offers is in France and is open only to French majors. Once you've started down the Spanish track, you're going to be stuck with it, so be careful when making such selections.

- If you need to work, you'll be forced to group your classes together so that you have blocks of time available to work. Many classes will be closed to you simply because of when they are scheduled. If you are in this situation, you have to be extra careful when making your decisions about which classes to select because you will have very little leeway to correct any mistakes.

STUDY HABITS

While your professors are an important part of each class, the real key is the effort you put into your courses. When you were in high school, you may have been given daily assignments that had to be done, and then your parents were probably looking over your shoulder to see that you were doing homework instead of goofing off. That type of supervision doesn't exist in a college setting, and many students abuse this freedom in the beginning of their first semester, only to discover the mistake they made by the end of the term.

If you thought you had a lot of distractions at home—television, the phone, and computer games—they don't compare to college life. There will still be TV, phones, and games, but there'll also be your roommate(s) and an entirely new style of living called dorm life. There will be many temptations not to study, and you have to learn to fend them off. The students who usually do best are those who come to college with the most focus. It's automatically assumed that a student who is on the premed track will study hard and do well. In fact, other students will be less likely to disturb those students because they know the obstacles they face. It would help your academic career immensely if you were shown the same respect, no matter what career path you've chosen, or even if you have no idea, but it's up to you to make it happen.

I'm sure you've heard the old saying that first impressions count. It certainly applies in this situation. If during the first few weeks of college you give every appearance of being a serious student, then you'll be taken for one, by your roommate, your fellow students, and your professors. And if you come on as Joe Party, there's a good chance that the reputation will stick throughout the four years you're in college.

> **Q.** When I was in high school, I got good grades, but I always boasted that I never had to study. I'd tell my friends that I watched TV all night, and while I might have had the TV on, so that I could know what was happening on the shows everyone watched, I also had a book open on my lap. The workload in college is even heavier and since I want to get good grades, I have to spend a lot of time hitting the books. Here's my problem. My three roommates are all buddies from high school. They always used to hear

me boast about how little I studied. I'm afraid that if they see me studying like crazy now, they're going to realize I was BSing them in high school and hate me for it. How do I save my reputation and still manage to keep my grades up?

A. Though I shouldn't encourage you to play with the truth again, it does seem to be a way out of your situation, and you also seem to have a talent for it. This time you should exaggerate how difficult the work is. Your friends will make fun of you, I'm sure, but at least you won't be blowing your cover for the hard work you put in during high school. It will give them some extra gratification to see you working, and maybe even inspire them to work harder. After some time has passed, you may even earn a new reputation for yourself—that of a hard worker.

There's a funny thing about reputations. They don't only affect others, they also affect you. Just as others expect you to live up to your reputation, be it nerd or class clown or Mr. Macho or cheerleader, you end up doing the same. You can actually become the stereotype that you create for yourself. If you think about this, you probably know it's true. If everybody thought about you in a certain way in high school, you tended to act that way, whether you wanted to or not. If you were known to always fool around and then tried to act serious one day, no one would believe it, and because of peer pressure, pretty soon you'd be your "old" self again.

But in college you won't have a reputation, so you have the opportunity to be whatever you want to be. Now I know it's easy to fall back on what you've always been doing, but we are so rarely offered a clean slate in life that it's very important for you to think this through ahead of time. If there are any bad habits you've picked up that you want to get rid of, entering college is the perfect opportunity to do so because no one will know about these habits, and so no one will push you toward taking them up. Is it easy to suddenly become very studious when up to now maybe all you've done is the bare minimum amount of schoolwork? No, but at least it's possible. So don't go off to college without a game plan. Decide ahead of time what you want out of college and go for it.

TIPS

- It's much easier to start out working as hard as you can than taking the easy way out and then trying to build up a head of steam. Don't be afraid to challenge yourself with hard classes, and make certain you let everybody around you know that you have a goal you're going to be working toward.

- Devote some time every day to organizing yourself. Write down what you need to do, putting down a date or time by when it needs to be done. And don't forget to consult that list, or it will be useless.

- Don't put off writing papers and other long-term projects to the last minute. What tends to happen is that everything ends up being due at the end of the semester, just when you should be studying for finals. Since you can't do everything at once, your grades will definitely suffer if you haven't worked on those papers ahead of time.

- Not everyone can get a 4.0 average, but too many students do poorly their first semester in college, and then have to work extra hard just to get their average up to the level they should be at. Be extra careful when you start out not to fall behind and then give up. As soon as you notice any slippage in your grades from what you were expecting, take whatever steps are necessary to begin getting them heading in an upward direction.

- If you find that you cannot cope with a particular class, don't just flounder by yourself. Ask for help. Colleges don't like to admit that they made a mistake with any one student, so they'll provide you with the assistance you need, but you have to ask for it.

6

THE DATING SCENE IN THE
NEW MILLENNIUM

While the main purpose of going to college is to get an education, no one can deny that what's also on almost everyone's mind is finding a significant other. Of course many young people going off to college have a boyfriend or girlfriend back home, but even those "coupled" people, faced with an entire campus full of new, bright, interesting, and mostly single people their own age, wonder what it would be like to go out with somebody new.

EXISTING RELATIONSHIPS

There are people who marry their high school sweetheart and go on to live happily ever after. As you will soon find out, however, there is a vast difference between a high school senior and a college senior. All students do a lot of growing up while they're in college and with both partners changing so much, it can be difficult to keep the flame of a high school romance alive, especially if the physical distance between you makes personal visits few and far between. While I'm not suggesting that everyone already in a relationship before they go off to college should break up with their boyfriend or girlfriend, I am saying that everyone needs some room to grow.

You should tell yourself that if the relationship is going to last, it has to make it on its own. You can't be overly clingy or overly jealous either. Maybe he or she needs to go out with a few other people to see how wonderful you are. Or maybe you'll both grow in the same direction and your relationship will strengthen. But it's also possible that like a caterpillar, you're meaning to shed this old relationship so that you can grow into a butterfly.

TIPS

- Definitely stay in touch with your boyfriend or girlfriend, but agree ahead of time that you won't talk every night on the telephone. Nor will you pry about every second of the other person's day. Giving the other person room to grow doesn't necessarily mean that you'll grow apart.

- Don't become hypersensitive. When two people are at a distance from each other, it's easy to misinterpret what is going on, so don't spend hours thinking about what one sentence in your last conversation meant. It's a useless exercise that will only drive you crazy.

- Don't string the other person along. Breaking up can be difficult, but if you've decided that the time has come to date other people, you must tell your boyfriend or girl-friend as soon as possible. It doesn't mean you've broken up forever, only that your relationship is in hiatus.

MAKING CONNECTIONS

In the not so distant past, fathers decided who their offspring would marry and no questions were asked. As society started to become more complex, young people were able to take more control of the mate-picking process, though for many years the underlying meaning of accepting even one invitation to dinner was that the two of you were going to be married. And when a date did occur, there was al-ways a chaperone to make sure that nothing more meaningful than an intense look passed between the two single people. Eventually dating became an accepted activity without any commitment, and today even marriage is not the final relationship it once was. But despite all these changes, the need that a human being has to be paired off with another hasn't really changed. All these permutations are simply ways of seeking the best possible relationship, and we are still far from having figured out how to work this process perfectly.

> **Q.** It seems like people in our generation never go on formal dates. We just "hang out." Is chivalry dead among our generation? Are we still feminists if we want men to open doors for us and take us out?

> **A.** I know that one-on-one dates are taking place less frequently than in the past, and there are good and bad aspects to that trend. In order to develop a relationship, you do have to spend some time together as a couple so, forgetting about chivalry, dating is a good intermediate step in taking a relationship to a more intimate level. On the other hand, having people of both sexes initially go out in groups does remove a lot of the pressure of having to ask someone out on a date, which most often fell on men.

> As far as opening doors and other "acts of chivalry," I still enjoy them and hope they won't fade away entirely. If they must, however, as part of the trade women have had to make in order to receive full equality in our society, then I guess that's a small price to pay.

Today many young people aren't dating one on one as much as they used to but rather they tend to go out in groups. While this is a good way of getting to know people without committing yourself, ultimately it cannot fulfill the desire to form a meaningful relationship with one other person. If you have a very busy schedule and don't want to get involved with any one special person, that's quite all right, although sometimes love can find its way into your heart no matter how hard you try to fight it off.

In case you don't know by now, I'm old-fashioned and a square, so one area where I would suggest you not venture into is having sex with people with whom you have no relationship. Sometimes people think they can remain simply friends and still share a sexual relationship. Basically they are saying you satisfy my sexual needs and I'll satisfy yours but we won't fall in love. While I'm not saying it can't happen, all too often it doesn't work out as planned. One of the two people involved winds up falling in love with the other, because having sex with someone does bring you closer together both physically and emotionally, and if the other person can't reciprocate, then the friendship is not going to survive this turn of events.

Even if they are not having sex, I'm not sure if two young people of the opposite sex can spend a lot of time together without at least one of them forming an emotional attachment to the other. Not wanting to risk damaging the friendship by openly declaring their love, the person in love may hide his or her feelings. It's even possible that each of them might be in love with the other at separate times.

I suppose what I'm saying is, there is such a strong desire in each of us to form a bond with another individual that it is almost inevitable for such pairings to occur when people are in close proximity. Actually, for the continuation of our species, that's a good thing, but it's a reality that must be put into your planning. It's easy to say you only want to be friends, but very often it doesn't quite work out that way.

PREDATORS

Some people take advantage of the looseness in the current dating scene. It's usually men, but some women are predators too. The only thing these people are interested in is "the hunt." They enjoy the process of luring other people into having sex with them, and as soon as they've consummated the act, they move on to find new prey.

Some of these predators are open as to what their goal is, and then the decision to get involved or not is entirely yours. Some people willingly fall into their game because they enjoy the sense of danger that surrounds these people. They may wind up feeling hurt or used again and again, but they can't seem to stop themselves from going along. But other predators don't let on what their motives are. They'll say whatever it takes to make the other person think they really care. They're also not above using alcohol or drugs to get what they want.

The key to protecting yourself against a predator is to know that they get bored rather easily. If they can't get what they want quickly, they'll move on to another person with whom they think they'll have better luck. So, as long as you never engage in sex before allowing some time to pass, and make sure you don't get so drunk or stoned that you don't know what you're doing, then you can protect yourself from becoming just another notch on their bedpost.

THE LONELY HEARTS

One question I'm asked again and again concerns meeting people of the opposite sex. Some say they can make friends but they can't get the relationship to the next level. Others say they are too shy even to meet people of the opposite sex. Both groups fret that they are destined to remain alone for the rest of their lives.

Overcoming shyness can be difficult, but not everyone who sits waiting for the phone to ring is actually dealing with being too shy.

Case: Jacquie

Jacquie was a woman with whom I had worked on a project. She was very nice and very competent at what she did. She was also somewhat overweight, and when she asked to see me privately in my office to talk about the difficulties she had with men, I thought her weight would be the main topic of conversation. I couldn't have been more wrong.

Because I am a "celebrity," Jacquie thought that I must know every other celebrity in New York. She was desperate to date a very famous comedian and the reason that she had asked for an appointment was to ask me to arrange for the two of them to go out.

UNREALISTIC EXPECTATIONS

Let's forget Jacquie's weight problem for the moment. Let's suppose she was a perfect 10. Even then I wouldn't have been able to help her. Why would some famous man go out on a blind date when he could meet all the women he wanted on his own? It's one thing to fantasize about celebrities as long as you remember that's exactly what they are, fantasies. There were men who were interested in Jacquie, but she refused to go out with them because she only wanted this comedian.

Jacquie was an extreme case, I admit. But how many other people are out there who set their sights on the captain of the football team or the queen of the prom or Mr. Moneybags or somebody who is already involved with somebody else? They allow themselves to become addicted to unrequited love. They know they can never have the object of their desire, but rather than move on, they dig themselves further and further into a hole.

Q. I have this habit of falling in love with people who end up not loving me back. I become friends with a young woman and we hang out together for a few months. I form an emotional attachment, and when I let her know my feelings, she ends up running the other way. I'm sick of having this happen to me again and again. How can I stop being the victim of unrequited love?

A. That this has happened to you more than once could just be a run of bad luck, or it could be something that you are doing wrong. These friendships prove that you obviously have many good qualities as a friend. One would think that one of these women would also make the jump to thinking of you in a more romantic way. What exactly is preventing this is difficult for me to guess.

What I can suggest as the means of ending this string of unrequited loves is that you stop trying to make friends out of the girls you meet. If you meet a young lady that you like, make sure you let her know that you are attracted to her *as a woman* right away, and not just as a friend. You may have to deal with several rejections, but as you won't have invested so much into these relationships, they won't be quite as painful, nor will you waste as much time on them. Eventually you'll find someone who reciprocates those feelings.

Now it's certainly possible to see somebody who appeals to you and try as hard as you can to get their attention. Yoko Ono camped out in front of John Lennon's house for weeks but eventually she did get her man. However, while it's perfectly acceptable to set your sights on another individual and make a valid effort to win them over, at

TIPS

- Be realistic in your selection process. If you're a guy who is on the short side, and you continually try to date tall women, then you're making life extra difficult for yourself. If you included some shorter women in the mix, you might meet with more success.

- First impressions do count. If you insist on dressing sloppily, for example, that's going to turn off a large percentage of people you want to meet before you even open your mouth. The concept of dressing for success doesn't only apply to your work life. It also matters in your love life.

- Don't be caught up in the superficial qualities of other people. The best-looking person in the room may not be the nicest person, or the most intelligent or the funniest or even the sexiest. Keep an open mind when you meet someone for the first time and try to look for their better qualities. (And no, this does not contradict the tip above, because while there are some aspects of a person's appearance that they cannot control, there are others that they can.)

some point you have to assess your chances and if they're just about nil, then you have to move on. And not to some other person who will also be impossible to catch. You have to give yourself a realistic chance or you will wind up always seeking and never finding that special someone. If you are constantly trying to get closer to people and failing each and every time, you have to take a step back and assess what you are doing wrong.

GOING OVER THE TOP

Another mistake people make is to fall instantly in love with someone they recently met. Just because a person agrees to go out on a date with you does not mean they intend to marry you, or even go out with you again. You have to give the other person a chance to warm up to you. You can't force someone to like you. If you act desperate, if you put pressure on them to commit to a relationship that hasn't even formed yet, they're going to run the other way, not necessarily because they want to, but because you're forcing them. So try to keep your emotions in check until there actually is a relationship developing between you and this other person.

This same advice applies to meeting people in the first place. If you are presented with the opportunity to talk with someone of the opposite sex (or same sex if you're gay) and you come on too strong, that person is not going to react positively. They want some time to get to know you before they are going to take the next step. After all, isn't that what you would do? We all react in a similar manner to certain stimuli, so if you are doing something that would turn you off, then don't expect that it would succeed on somebody else.

This syndrome often occurs in people who haven't been out on a date in months, or even years. When someone finally pays attention to them, they immediately overreact. They start dreaming of marriage and act in ways that are inappropriate to the depth of the actual relationship. I understand that you might get very excited by some sudden attention, but if you can't keep your emotions to yourself, then you run the risk of alienating this person who has shown some willingness to develop a relationship.

If you're the type to react this way, you must get your emotions under control as quickly as possible. Under no circumstances can you allow yourself to start thinking too far ahead. Such daydreams are a luxury that you just cannot afford. And when you are with this person, you must be attentive to how you are reacting. If you start to gush, then quickly stop yourself. If you can't learn to rein in your emotions, there's a good chance that you'll keep driving people away.

THE WALLFLOWER SYNDROME

Of course you can't expect to meet people if you go to the other extreme and just sit in a corner. You do have to make an effort. The first step is to leave your dorm room. Sure a few people do drop in now and then, but it certainly limits your selection. If you're looking to meet a potential lover, you have to go to places where people are congregating—parties, concerts, rallies, sporting events, lectures, etc. Colleges have a full schedule of activities, and the more of them you attend, the more likely that you'll meet that special someone.

But, of course, just going to an event isn't all it takes. Historically men have been the one to initiate contact, so women may hesitate about being too forward. But even before the days of women's liberation, young ladies could make eye contact, or drop a handkerchief, so don't let your sex be an excuse.

Once both parties have signaled some interest through eye contact or in some other form of body language, like a smile or, for the bold, even a wink, communications have to be carried to the next level, meaning you have to talk to each other. Finding, first of all, the nerve to speak up, and then something to say seems to be a major stumbling block for some people, while for others it comes as naturally as breathing. If you're in the glib school, then you don't need any advice, but for those of you who end up tongue-tied, I'll give you some suggestions.

1. Avoid using trite lead-ins, like "Haven't I seen you here before?" It marks you as someone with little imagination.
2. Compliments, like "that's a pretty blouse you're wearing," are all right as icebreakers, but need back up, because the other person is going to say "Thanks," and then what?
3. If you're at an event that has some content, like a lecture or concert, rather than at a purely social event, it gives you the opportunity to comment on what's been going on, whether it be good or bad, and that can certainly lead to further conversation, which is why I advocate going to such places to meet people.
4. Read the newspaper, and not just the headlines. There may be a story on page 45 that would give you the perfect opening to say something clever.
5. Practice in front of a mirror or with a friend. Don't all your favorite actors and actresses rehearse their lines over and over again? Do you think you're better than they are? So you've got to rehearse too.
6. Have multiple interests. It's great to like sports or cooking, but if the other person doesn't share that interest, then where does the conversation go?
7. Jokes are okay, but don't lead anywhere. A string of jokes will only make you seem like a clown. My advice about jokes would be to memorize a few, but use them only if there is a lull in the conversation.
8. Make sure you ask the other person his or her name and use it a few times during the conversation so that you don't forget it. Also, since everyone at a college is listed in a directory, if the conversation doesn't last that long, for whatever reason, you'll have a way of contacting them later.
9. Names can also be an opening to further conversation. Let's say the other person's last name is clearly Italian. That might lead you to say all sorts of things, from talking about your background to asking how long ago the person's family came to the States to your favorite Italian restaurant.
10. Listen to what the other person is saying. In the first place, it

makes them feel good to know you care about their opinions, which they'll notice if you respond directly to what they've just said rather than go off on a tangent of your own. It also relieves some of your burden to keep the conversation humming along, as two people exchanging ideas both share in the responsibility.

11. Don't panic if there's moment of silence. Conversations have their ups and downs, but if you allow yourself to get too nervous about a small lapse, then you may never think of what to say to get things started again.

12. One way to break up a lull in the conversation is to suggest a move to somewhere else. It could just be over to the bar to get a drink, or to some chairs to sit down, or outside of where you are for some food, drinks, fresh air, or an atmosphere quiet enough to allow you to hold a conversation. This movement will indicate forward progress in the relationship, as well as give you both time to think of other things to say.

13. Don't reveal too much about yourself too quickly, especially your faults. There's no worse way to bore the other party than to discuss such issues as weight and diet and other personal problems.

14. College students have one easy topic of conversation: the classes they take. It's not the first thing you should talk about, but it can ease your way into deeper conversation if there's a moment of awkwardness.

15. If you're really uncomfortable in your own skin, perhaps you'd do better in somebody else's. Pretend that you're someone else, maybe somebody famous, a professor you admire or just your roommate, and act the part. I don't advise that you go over the top and start quoting scenes from a movie ("You talking to me!"). It shouldn't be obvious that you are role-playing, but rather just a means of helping you concentrate on making conversation, which as they say, is an art form. Try it out on a friend first and see if this method might make conversation easier for you.

16. Finally, there's always "Hi." Let's say you've made eye contact

with someone and it's clear that you're both interested in finding out more about each other. And let's say you're very shy
and because you are interested, you're more tongue-tied than
ever. There are two possibilities. One is that you turn away and
have absolutely no chance of getting to meet the other person.
The other is to walk over and say "Hi." Maybe your tongue will
stay permanently glued to the top of your palate and you'll look
like a fool, but you're no worse off than if you'd turned away.
On the other hand, maybe they'll say something in response
that will inspire you to answer back. You're not risking any
more by saying Hi than by walking away, and the payoff could
be far greater, so take my advice and be like that turtle who
sticks his neck out.

LIVING IN THE POST FEMINIST WORLD

Not too long ago there were certain rules regarding dating that everybody followed. One of the basics was that the guy asked the girl out.
All she was allowed to do was sit by the phone and wait. That has
changed and it's quite acceptable for a woman to be the initiator. But
while it's acceptable, it is not yet the norm, and so there can be problems of communication when it does occur.

There are going to be some men who, when asked out, are going
to assume that the woman is so turned on by him, or so desperate,
that she'll do anything, including having sex. These men might not be
interested in having a relationship, but if they think they can get some
casual sex, they'll say yes.

Of course there's also the other side of that coin. These men also
think that the woman wants to have sex, but not out of desperation,
but because she is the aggressive type. Rather than turning them on,
it scares them. They're used to being the ones to take the first step
and they can't handle having the tables turned.

And, of course, the poor woman may not be looking to hop into
the sack on the first date at all. Maybe she is merely looking for some
companionship and got tired of waiting for someone to ask her out.

Q. My roommate and I planned to go to a concert on campus. We bought our tickets in advance, but then she caught the flu and couldn't make it. Rather than waste the ticket, I asked this guy I had talked to occasionally in class. During the concert, he was all over me and afterward I couldn't get rid of him. Does a guy have a right to think that being asked out gives him a free pass?

A. I think what happened to you arose 10 percent from the situation and 90 percent because he doesn't have enough experience around women. In all probability you would not have asked a complete stranger or someone you didn't like, so the inference was that you did like him. But he took that one little signal and in his fantasies blew it up into an X-rated neon billboard and then tried to act them out without first finding out whether there was any substance to them.

If he had been the one to ask you to the concert, my guess is that you would have gone, and he still might have acted in the same manner, so you see it's not so much what you did, as the way he overreacted. You shouldn't let this one bad experience scare you away from ever approaching a man again. Even if many men might share the same fantasies he had, I doubt very many would automatically start to paw at you without getting some further signals from you.

Now if two people know each other and are friends, it should make the process easier, though there is always the chance of miscommunication. That's why a woman must make her intentions as clear as possible, and be careful not to get herself into a situation that would be embarrassing to both parties. For example, if you've asked someone out to a concert, make sure your roommate is in your room when you return so that if he insists on walking you to your room, there'll be no chance of things getting out of hand.

I might also suggest that such an invitation might be easier if it is to be part of a group. In other words, if you and some friends have made plans to go into town to see a movie, and you ask a guy you like to join all of you, you'll have signaled your intention of wanting to be with him without making it appear more serious than that.

DATE RAPE

Date rape exists, there is no question about that, and it is always wrong. But I believe that certain instances of date rape are avoidable on the part of the woman. Her actions may not give a man license to rape her, but on the other hand, they do increase the chances of her being raped and so should be avoided.

What I am talking about, mainly, is going too far, in one form or another. If a young woman goes out with a man and drinks to the point of almost passing out, she is making the possibility of being raped much more likely. This is especially true if he has also been drinking.

Another way a woman can go too far is to get completely undressed with a man and lie down on a bed with him. A man who would never think of ripping off her clothes and forcibly raping her might, in the heat of passion, not be able to resist the temptation of slipping his penis inside her vagina. Just the act of the man trying to remove her panties would be enough of a signal to her that things had gotten out of hand and she could probably stop a rape from occurring. But if both are completely naked, lying next to one another, then intercourse might take place before she could prevent it. And if you combine the two, alcohol or drugs, and nudity, then the possibility of a rape occurring increases even more.

In my opinion, any woman who allows herself to get into one of these situations is contributing to her own rape. Now, if she is so aroused that she willingly takes all her clothes off, expecting that he is going to give her an orgasm one way or the other, the unplanned intercourse, even if it meant the loss of her virginity, would be sad, but in this era of sexual liberation not the end of the world. But a rape means that she is unprotected, and could cause an unintended pregnancy or give her a sexually transmitted disease, which could even be deadly. These consequences are truly frightening, which is why I counsel every woman to avoid putting herself at risk.

SAYING NO

Certainly any woman would say no to being raped, given the chance, but turning down a date, or being turned down for a date, is not so simple an action as it may appear, or at least shouldn't be if you have any concern for your fellow human beings. And since women can now be the ones doing the asking, men have to share the same concerns.

The tricky part about saying no is that, assuming you want that door closed for good, you want to let the other person know that they have no chance, but you also don't want to put them down personally. The way I see things, there's nothing wrong with white lies. White lies are told to avoid causing pain to another person. So instead of telling someone that you don't want to date them, it might be better to tell them that you're permanently unavailable. At college that can be relatively easy because all you have to do is say you have a "significant other" back home and you've promised each other not to date. If this person then does see you out with other people, it may be a little awkward, but if they do confront you, you can always say circumstances have changed.

You could also say that you've just broken up with somebody and you're not ready to date yet. Or that your grades need to be raised so that you don't lose your scholarship and you don't have the time to go out.

If you are morally against even white lies, then I would say to keep it simple and don't give a reason, even if pressed. After all, the main reason people refuse an offer for a date, since they probably don't know the person that well, is that they have a superficial negative reaction to the person asking. Since there's no "nice" way of communicating that, it is better left unsaid.

And what if you are the person being rejected? How should you react? My advice is to realize that there are people with whom you would not want to go out, and if you have the right to say no to them, then so does the person you've asked. To say "don't take it personally" is silly, because it usually is a personal rejection. But just as everyone doesn't appeal to you, you can't possibly appeal to everyone, and that's just part of life.

What if you're always being rejected? As we noted before, there are people who complain they can never get a date. We dealt with those people who are too shy to ask someone out, but there are others who do ask, and get constantly rejected. What they might be doing wrong and how they can correct it is our next topic.

TIPS

- If you feel that your looks aren't your strong point, but your personality is, then seek out people to date who are in the same category you are.

- Try to do the most possible with your looks. Wear clothes that compliment your size and shape. Spend a little extra to get the best hair style. Compare your wardrobe to what is being featured in the fashion magazines and make any needed adjustments.

- If you're not sure how others perceive you, ask a friend or two to give you an honest opinion. Ask them particularly if there is anything that you could do to improve how people see you.

- If being overweight is your problem, vow to do something about it. Don't aim for extremes, but rather make small changes, in terms of eating habits and exercise, that you can easily integrate into your lifestyle and will yield long-lasting results.

- Some people will only go out with others who are in the same social class they perceive themselves to be in. The fact is that they are missing out on meeting a lot of very good people, so don't feel badly about not being right for this group. Instead, think better of yourself for not sharing their attitude.

As we already covered, there are some people who shoot too high, only asking dates of people who are unlikely to want to date them. It may not be pleasant to accept, but there are pecking orders in every society, and you have to take stock of where you fit in, and act accordingly. If the young ladies on the cheerleading squad are all looking to date some of the athletes, and you're not on the team, then if the only people you ask out are cheerleaders, you're not going to ever get a date.

COMMUNICATION ISSUES

Let's say that you have been trying to date people, most of whom should be willing to consider going out with you, but you're batting zero. Or that you're really want to go out on dates, but nobody is calling you and you're not willing to risk asking. Is there hope for you, or are you destined to go through the rest of your life without a partner?

Before I deal with this issue, let me give you an example—me. As you may be aware, I am only 4'7". When I was younger, I was certain that my height would prevent me from ever finding a husband. And not only was I short, I was a poor orphan whose only formal training was how to be a housekeeper. Looking objectively at my situation, I thought my prospects were dim. As it turned out, my worries were baseless because I ended up married three times (the last time for thirty five years until my husband passed away a few years ago).

So how did I overcome the obstacles that I had obsessed about? I have a very strong personality, and maybe because I am so short, I work hard to let people know that I am there. Of course each person is different, so what worked for me might not be appropriate for you, but the basic notion is the same; accentuate your assets, whatever they might be. I'll give you some specific examples of what you might do.

1. If you're good in a particular subject, and you notice someone whom you might like to be friends with floundering a bit in

class, find a way of offering that person your help in this subject. Maybe you can explain a particularly difficult aspect. Or help with an assignment. Once you've given your assistance, who knows what might happen next.

2. If you play the guitar, set yourself up in an area where lots of people pass by and just start playing. The odds are some people will stop and listen, and you can make new friends this way, one of whom may turn out to be someone special.

3. If you're good at organizing, organize some group activity. Since you started it, you're bound to be included, and who knows whom you might meet. And if the first thing you try to organize bombs, then wait a few weeks and try again, doing some additional homework to find an event that will be more popular.

4. If you're a good writer, put up some notices that say you're willing to help people who need help with writing. Just by putting yourself into a situation where you are meeting people will increase your chances of meeting someone whom you can then date.

5. If you know how to sew, offer your services by posting notes around campus. There are probably plenty of people, guys in particular, who are desperate to have some repairs done and don't have a clue what to do.

MEETING PEOPLE

If you were "good enough" to be accepted into your college, then you can be certain that there are probably hundreds of other people on campus who are on a par with you in many ways and who are potential partners. What you have to do is meet enough people on campus until you make the right connection. Even if you are a super model or champion athlete, you won't meet anyone if all you do is sit in your room. The more people you meet, the better your chances of meeting a potential partner, so here are some ways to widen the scope of people with whom you interact.

1. Tell everyone you know that you're interested in meeting someone. Networking almost always yields results, and even if you
   end up meeting a few people that aren't right for you, if you go
   through the process with a positive attitude, you should come
   out ahead.

2. Get to know your RA, and then pump him or her for information about other students who might be right for you. Remember, RAs for your floor know many of the other RAs on campus
   so they're a good network to tap into.

3. Go to religious services and volunteer to take part in whatever
   ways you can, for example singing with the choir.

4. If there is a crisis somewhere where people require relief, like
   an earthquake or flood, organize a fund-raising effort. That will
   help you meet lots of new people.

5. Conduct a survey. Say it's for the school newspaper (which will
   probably accept it even if they haven't assigned it to you). That
   will give you "permission" to speak to hundreds of students.
   Just be as friendly as possible and you never know what you may
   learn.

6. Go to as many organized events as you possibly can. Most campuses have many going on every week. These give you a chance
   to meet new people as well as run into those you already know.

7. Speak up in your classes. Obviously you shouldn't blurt out just
   anything, but if you make some intelligent comments, it's sort
   of like free advertising to all of your classmates.

8. Do go to some purely social events, for example, parties. Many
   people meet this way and it would be unwise for you to put
   yourself above the fray, as it were. I would recommend that you
   don't go with a large group of friends. If your aim is to meet
   new people, you might even be better off alone. Since you'll be
   embarrassed to be standing there by yourself, it will force you
   to interact with those around you.

9. And if the weather is nice and there are loads of students out
   and about, just going for a walk can sometimes be effective.
   Walk slowly, so that you have a chance to see who is around you,
   and with your eyes up, so that if there's a chance to make eye

contact, you can. And if you're a female, I suggest you bring a book. People don't carry hankies any more, but if you "accidentally" drop your book, it can be just as effective.

LEFT AT THE ALTAR

What happens if you do meet somebody, go out for a time, and then he or she decides to move on? Even if the feeling is mutual—even if you end up hating each other—breaking up remains hard to do.

The most important thing to remember about a feeling of loss, and that includes dealing with breaking up, divorce, or losing a family member, is that you cannot forget what happened. Many people make the mistake of thinking they can bury all their feelings about this tragic event, and when that happens they'll be able to move on. But since you can't forget, and you can't erase all the memories, following this course of action means that you can never get on with your life.

But just because you can't forget doesn't mean that you can't move on. Your goal should be to make those memories less painful. You have to allow yourself to be sad for a time, and eventually your emotions will start to heal. But if you try to bury those emotions, then they can never heal and you can't get past them. As long as you remember this, you can deal with whatever sad moments occur in your life. Just say to yourself they're supposed to be sad, and allow yourself to be sad for a time. Then the natural healing process will take over and while you may never be "good as new," you can definitely come close to being your old self.

7

SEX

Need I Say More? Yes!

A great many young people have sexual intercourse for the first time while they are in college. I purposefully didn't say that they had sex, because quite a few of those students who considered themselves virgins before they got to college had engaged in petting or outercourse, where they gave each other orgasms manually or by rubbing their bodies together, and in oral sex. While there are certainly greater risks that come with having intercourse, primarily the risk of an unintended pregnancy as well as an increased risk of a sexually transmitted disease, the satisfaction that comes from an orgasm that occurs during intercourse is not so much different from one that comes through other means. In fact, many young women, who were having orgasms before they started having intercourse, may find that those orgasms are harder to come by during intercourse. But I'm jumping ahead of myself here, though I promise that I will deal with that issue further on in this chapter.

I'm going to presume that since you're in college, you were given a high school course in human sexuality as well as a course in biology, so that you are familiar with the very basics about sex. But while your high school courses may have done a good job explaining about how babies are made, they rarely go into the details of how to have good sex, by which I mean pleasurable sex.

Q. I tried out for the chorus because I figured there would be a lot of girls and I'd meet some. I got selected and after our first rehearsal this senior (I'm a freshman) started talking to me, and one thing led to another and the next thing you know we were having sex. I was a virgin and I hadn't planned on losing my virginity so quickly, but she came on really strong and I just couldn't say no. She seemed to really enjoy it, but afterward I felt used, and now I sort of regret having given it up so easily, especially as the next time I saw her, she barely acknowledged me. What do I do now?

A. That's a sad story but it's not the end of the world. Yes, you were used, but don't allow what happened to affect you forever. The important thing is not just putting your penis into a vagina. Lots of men have done that for the first time with a prostitute. You still have the opportunity to make love for the first time with someone you really care for, so just make sure that when that happens, you make it as special as you always imagined it would be.

Now since I'm old-fashioned and a square, to me sex is something that should only be engaged in by two people who care for each other. There should be a strong relationship, and having sex should be an expression of their love for each other. Of course I realize that not every sexual episode follows these conditions. Many people do engage in casual sex, and I've even visited a house of prostitution where money was the only reason sex occurred. But while one can certainly derive pleasure from sex, that is not part of a *relationship*. It's more difficult to have terrific sex and it's harder to treat sexual dysfunctions under these conditions. That's because sex that occurs as an expression of love has some added dimensions. So I would encourage you to have sex only when you are part of a committed couple. Of course I can't force you to listen to me, but much of the advice I am going to give may help you whether you are in a serious relationship or not.

THE BIGGEST PROBLEMS

I'm often asked by reporters what are the most common questions
people ask of me. When it comes to sexual functioning, there are two,
one for each sex as it turns out. For men, it concerns premature ejaculation. For women, it's the inability to have an orgasm. Since they
are common problems, or for those of you who are still virgins, common fears, I'll start out with what I have to say about each of them,
using them as platforms to discuss sexual functioning in general.

Premature Ejaculation

To begin with, what is premature ejaculation? PM occurs when a
man can't stop himself from having an orgasm during intercourse.
Where this poses the most difficulty is when the man ejaculates
during the first few minutes of intercourse, or even before he can
penetrate the woman. But even if he can last thirty minutes and at
that point can't stop himself, it is still premature ejaculation. On the
other hand, if a man ejaculates after only a minute because he wants
to, and could have lasted longer, then that is not premature ejaculation.

There are many theories as to why some men have this inability. A
common theory is that young boys must learn to masturbate quickly
in order not to get caught and then they have problems unlearning
this ability. We don't know whether this is true, but the concept that
it is a learning disability is correct. Any man can teach himself to control his ability to ejaculate, and that's the good news, as no man needs
to remain a premature ejaculator forever.

Basically what a man must learn is to recognize the premonitory
sensation. Those are the feelings just before he passes the point when
there is no stopping that orgasm. If he can learn to identify those sensations, then all he has to do is calm himself down a bit, and the urge
to have an orgasm will be under his control. It usually takes a few
sessions to learn to do this, and it is better done with a willing partner,
though a man could practice on his own.

TIPS

- Don't assume that because you masturbate quickly you will have problems with premature ejaculation. Going in with a positive attitude is very important in every aspect of good sexual functioning.

- A key point to keep in mind is that many women cannot have an orgasm through intercourse alone. While the desire to keep intercourse going for more than a minute or two is natural, the ability to control your orgasms for an unlimited amount of time may still not be enough to give a woman an orgasm.

- To get more detailed information on how to deal with premature ejaculation, try looking it up in a book that deals only with sex. If you can't learn the proper technique only by reading a book, then go to see a sex therapist.

It is definitely more difficult to learn this technique when you are having intercourse with someone you barely know. Under those circumstances, a man is going to be worried about his performance and that is not what we educators call a teachable moment. So here's a case in point where having a relationship can be vital to a man's sexual functioning.

Erectile Difficulties

Sometimes a man worries so much about his skills at pleasing a woman that it interferes with his ability to obtain or maintain an erection. The worries block out the pleasant feelings and his penis goes limp and stubbornly refuses to rise to the occasion, as it were. And the more the man worries about it, the more difficult it is for him to get over this problem. Again, if he has an understanding partner, he can take his time, as well as know that if it doesn't work this time, there will be a next time with this same woman because she wants to be with him and not with anyone else. That's an ego boost that no amount of psychotherapy can match. But if he is going from woman to woman, the fear that he will have erectile difficulties can become so great that it becomes a self-fulfilling prophecy. The longer this lasts, the harder it will be to get over.

And by the way, this is not an occasion for a young man to resort to Viagra or any other drug. These drugs were made to help men with a physical disability. If a man with erectile difficulty wants to have an erection and can't, then these pills can be quite helpful. But if a man cannot obtain an erection because of a psychological problem, drugs are not going to help him.

The Preorgasmic Woman

There was a time when a woman who couldn't have an orgasm was called frigid. That was terrible because it put all of the onus on *her*, which was inaccurate. Today we call such women preorgasmic, because unless a woman has a particular physical disorder, helping any woman to have orgasms is not that difficult.

I mentioned a bit earlier that many women cannot have an orgasm through intercourse alone. The reason for this is that all orgasms are caused by stimulation to the woman's clitoris, and since the clitoris is situated at the top of the vagina, where it can be protected during childbirth, many women do not get sufficient stimulation to their clitoris by the penis during intercourse to cause an orgasm.

By the way, it is not the size of the male apparatus that is usually at fault here. The nerve endings in a woman's vagina are all concentrated at the outer third, so that the size of the penis is really not that important to most women. Yes, there are women to whom the sensation of being "filled" by a large penis is something she needs to be fully satisfied, and these women will gravitate to men with larger members. But to most women, as long as the man's penis is not minuscule, it just doesn't matter. In fact, there are women who find it painful to have intercourse with a man who has a very large penis. However, most men would be better off not worrying about the size of their penis, but instead make sure that their knowledge about how to please a woman is at its maximum level.

FOREPLAY

I hope all of you have heard of foreplay, although you may not know exactly what it means. While both partners derive a great deal of pleasure from touching and hugging and kissing each other prior to intercourse, during foreplay many women receive the clitoral stimulation they require in order to have an orgasm. Some women can only have an orgasm if their clitoris is being directly stimulated, while others can become sufficiently aroused during foreplay that they can then have an orgasm during intercourse.

When I used the word intercourse in the sentence above, what you probably pictured was two people in the missionary position, that is to say, with the woman lying down and the man on top of her. While that is the most common position for intercourse, and the one usually depicted in the movies, it is the worst position for a woman to have an orgasm because the man cannot stimulate her clitoris when they are in this position. There are many other positions where it is very easy for the man to touch the woman's clitoris during intercourse. Two of the most commonly used ones are the female superior position, where the women is on top, and the side to side position. These positions make it much more likely that she can have an orgasm while his penis is inside her vagina, a sensation that many women enjoy, rather than to have an orgasm either before or after intercourse. Some men also find that they have more control over their orgasms in these positions, so that may be another benefit.

Case: Laurie

I've been going out with my boyfriend for almost a year. We love each other very much and he'll do anything to please me. The problem is that I can't seem to have an orgasm no matter what he does. He uses his finger and he goes down on me for hours, and nothing works. We're both very frustrated by this. In fact, he may be more frustrated than me. I'm sort of willing to give up on ever enjoying sex, but he insists that he's going to figure out a way to make me have an orgasm. What can I do? Maybe I should just start faking it.

While you now know that the woman needs to have her clitoris stimulated, exactly how this should be done to be most effective is not the same for every woman. Sometimes the couple can explore various means together in order to get the answer, and sometimes the woman must learn how to give herself an orgasm first, and then teach the man what techniques work best for her. The reason for this is that having another person there—the man—can be distracting to the woman. If she has never had an orgasm, she may need her full concentration in order to learn what works best for her, and so masturbation is the only means of doing this.

TIPS

- Don't assume that direct contact on the clitoris is what is going to work. Some women need to only be touched around their clitoris as they find direct contact too stimulating.

- Many women find flowing water provides the right sensations to produce an orgasm. One source could be one of those handheld showers sprayed against her clitoris. Or she could lie down in the tub, placing her buttocks up against the wall of the tub so that the water flowing out of the tub's faucet falls directly on her clitoris.

- If a woman does not produce sufficient natural lubrication, she shouldn't hesitate to use an articifical lubricant because the pain resulting from any irritation caused by excessive friction will make it more difficult for her to have an orgasm.

I know there are women who say they just cannot bring themselves to masturbate. They were taught that this activity is dirty and it bothers them to touch their own genitals. Men don't seem to have this problem as much, perhaps because they are far more used to handling their penis, given that they do so every time they urinate. While

I understand women's reticence, their excuse may not be valid. Certainly people fear surgery, but if they need it to restore their health, then they find the courage to go under the knife. Because masturbation involves pleasure, it is guilt rather than fear that has to be overcome, but the same principle is involved. If a woman is going to remain unorgasmic her entire life, not only will she suffer, but so will any man with whom she becomes involved in a relationship.

Q. When I first got my period, my mother sat me down and explained the facts of life, at least her version of them. She told me about sex, and told me it would hurt, but that I had to endure it if I wanted children. Because of that I was terrified of ever having sex, and though boys would ask me out, I didn't want to even date because I was so afraid that we might have sex. Eventually I learned the truth, but I can't quite shake the fear. Whenever I start to get close to a man, I end up pulling away so that we never get to the point of having sex. Am I never going to have sex?

A. If you had no idea of what was going on, then perhaps you could never overcome this problem, but since you know exactly the cause of your difficulties, you absolutely can overcome this. You've already made the first step by asking me this question.

The next time you are going out with a man, if he seems like someone you could really love, and if he is really a "nice" guy, then at some point you should tell him your predicament. You can't do it right at the moment when you might be going to have sex. If passions are high, you are very scared, and he is very aroused, it will be very difficult for the two of you to overcome this issue. But once you know you would like to have sex with him, if you let him know ahead of time that you have this problem and you talk it out, then I think it is much more likely that together you can arrive at a solution. And if it turns out that you can't handle it on your own, then I would suggest that you consult a sex therapist before you lose this man.

It used to be that women would endure intercourse in order to have babies, but now both men and women know that such fortitude is not necessary. Men have realized that they derive much pleasure from giving their partners an orgasm and that lovemaking offers much more when both partners can fully share in the enjoyment.

THE VIBRATOR

When all else has failed, what can often help a woman become orgasmic is a device known as a vibrator. Vibrators offer two benefits. First of all, the woman need not touch her genitals directly. But more importantly, they create intense sensations that can help a woman have a successful orgasm.

The only drawback to using a vibrator is that the sensations can be so strong that a woman might become so used to them that she cannot have an orgasm without one. Now if a vibrator turns out to be the only way a woman can have an orgasm, there's nothing wrong with that. But most couples prefer the man to have more of a role to play, so I usually advise women not to use a vibrator exclusively.

TIPS

- Because of the intense sensations created by vibrators, many women do not place the tip of the vibrator directly on their clitoris, but around it, which causes enough sensations to give them an orgasm.

- Some vibrators come with different attachments that can be placed on the head of the device, to give different types of sensations.

- In order not to become completely reliant on a vibrator to give you an orgasm, from time to time give yourself an orgasm without using the vibrator at all, or use the vibrator to arouse you, but then finish giving yourself an orgasm with your hand.

TIPS

- Some vibrators are shaped like a penis, so that they can be inserted into the woman's vagina as well as used to stimulate the clitoris, while others are not. If a woman wants to also feel the sensations that come from having something inside of her vagina, she could use a dildo, an artificial penis, or some other object, to take the place of the penis.

THE FIRST TIME

Since many college students are virgins, here is some advice about the first time you have intercourse. I would like to begin by lowering your expectations. That may seem cruel of me, but actually I am doing you a favor. We've all seen people going at it forcefully in the movies, and many of us have read a love scene in a book where the "earth moves" for the two lovers. But just the way the movies show people walking away from car crashes or surviving a twister, fictional lovemaking does not necessarily replicate real life. And that's especially true of your first time, whether both of you are newcomers to the game or only one.

Remember the first time you picked up a basketball or tennis racquet? You weren't very good, were you? Or the first time you tried to make dinner for the family? How tasty was it? There are so many things in life that you can't do perfectly the first time, and the rule "practice makes perfect" applies to sexual intercourse as well.

Based on this fact, I have a whole litany of reasons why your "first time" should not be with some stranger. First of all, it's not going to be all that sexually satisfying. He may be too excited and reach orgasm too fast. She might not have an orgasm at all. So you'll want more opportunities to perfect your skills with the same partner. And if you're going to be awkward about doing something new, it certainly is better to fumble around with someone you love and who loves you and who won't be anywhere near as judgmental as a stranger might be. And, finally, you'll never forget your first time, so wouldn't it be much better if you could attach this experience to a name and a face you associate with good feelings rather than with someone who's got a giant question mark where their face should be?

All right, so now you've got the right partner and you're going to do "it" for the first time, what is it that you have to know, besides that somehow or other the man's penis has to go inside the woman's vagina?

1. It's important that the man's penis be hard. That may sound obvious, but if for whatever reason—fear being the key concern—his penis is not hard, then it's going to be very difficult, if not impossible, to complete the act and it probably shouldn't be attempted. (Another cause for a man's inability to have an erection could be too much alcohol or drugs, or even too much food. So if you know that "tonight's the night," keep all consumptions, of whatever variety, to a moderate level.)

2. There has to be enough lubrication. If the woman is scared, then she won't be excited, and if she's not excited, she won't lubricate. Trying to stick a penis into a dry vagina is tough even for those with plenty of expertise, but for newbies, it's going to be impossible. If she's too dry, stop everything until you can get an articifical lubricant. (And bear in mind, if you're using a condom, don't apply any petroleum product, such as Vaseline, because it eats through latex.)

3. The next important point is to make sure you are protected. If one or both of you are worried about the potential consequences of this first time, those worries are going to ensure that it will not be a very pleasurable experience. If you are both virgins, then an unintended pregnancy is all that you are concerned about. If one of you is experienced, sexually transmitted diseases also must be considered. Condoms protect against both, but are not 100 percent reliable.

4. Here I'd like to kill two myths. One is that a woman can't get pregnant her first time. It's absolutely not true, and many women learn this the hard way. The second is that the withdrawal method is an effective method of birth control. That

isn't true either. Before a man ejaculates, there is some liquid that appears at the tip of his penis. It's called Cowper's fluid and it serves as a lubricant for the sperm to come, but it is full of sperm and can cause pregnancy. So even if he does pull out before he ejaculates, which doesn't always happen no matter how much he promises, she will still have had thousands of sperm placed inside her vagina. And how many does it take to make her pregnant? One, or as I like to say, one fast one.

5. Penetration is sometimes easier if the angle of intromission is changed—the angle at which the penis is inserted. To do this, the woman should place a pillow underneath her buttocks.

6. In the movies, the man gets on top of the woman and right away they start moving up and down. With the exception of porn films, that happens because the man doesn't really stick his penis inside of her vagina. They're simulating sex. In real life, the penis doesn't always just slip inside on its own. Sometimes it needs a little guidance. If the couple is in the missionary position, where the man is holding himself up with his arms, he doesn't have any available hands with which to steer, so it's up to the woman to spread her vaginal lips apart and point the penis in the right direction. In other positions the man can use his own hands to guide his penis where it has to go.

7. Women are born with a layer of skin that covers the opening of the vagina. It's called the hymen (aka the cherry). When the hymen is first broken, it causes some bleeding, and in olden times, the bloody sheets were put on display the morning after the honeymoon to show the world that the new bride was truly a virgin. Those days are gone, and so are the hymen of many women, who break it when playing sports or bicycle riding. There is some pain involved in breaking the hymen for the first time during intercourse, but it is not overwhelming and is nothing to be afraid of, though the expectation of this pain is one more reason why many women do not achieve sexual satisfaction their first time.

8. Fear can cause pain of another sort, called vaginismus. If a

woman is afraid of having intercourse, her vaginal muscles may tighten up involuntarily. This makes it impossible for the man to place his penis inside of her, and he might cause her some pain in trying. She might calm down with a gentle lover and this condition will go away on its own, but if for some reason it doesn't, then medical attention is called for.

9. There are other pressures that can make sex impossible or not very pleasurable, especially the first time. One pressure stems from not having enough time or privacy. I recognize that many people have lost their virginity in the backseat of a car, but if the lovers are trying to rush through this initial episode and are looking over their shoulders to make sure that they're not caught in the beam of some policeman's flashlight, then that is not going to be conducive to good sexual functioning. Any time you have sex, but especially the first time, try to do it in a place where you are protected from prying eyes, and at a time when you are not rushed.

10. Orgasms and the first time. While there is a good chance the man is going to have an orgasm his first time having sex, it is much less likely that the woman will. She's going to be nervous about any potential pain, and emotional about losing her status of being a virgin, which even if not as valued as it once was, is still important even in the twenty-first century. I would not advise young men to try to force their partners to have an orgasm. If she says that she's not interested, leave it at that. Sometimes a person has only so much capacity for strong emotions, and if she's feeling very moved by losing her virginity, her capacity to have an orgasm may just not be there.

Let's assume that you have successfully completed your first sexual union. Do you wonder: Is that all there is to it? Do you qualify as an expert from doing it once, or even twice? I think you know the answer to that, and while this is not a sex book per se, there are a few more tips that I'd like to pass on just to cover the bare minimum knowledge you need. (Actually, if you are soon to become sexually active for the first time, I would highly recommend that you read an entire book on the subject, or maybe even more than one. Highly recommended are *The Joy of Sex* and *More Joy of Sex* by Alex Comfort. Another is a little tome that happens to bear my name, which is titled *Sex for Dummies*.)

AFTERPLAY

Afterplay is a concept that is not as widely known as foreplay, but to women it is almost as important. Men tend to get aroused very easily, and then come down from that aroused state just as quickly after they've had their orgasm. Women, on the other hand, take longer to become aroused, and then, after they've had their orgasm, take longer to descend to their normal state. To a woman, being hugged and caressed and having sweet nothings whispered in her ear after she's had her orgasm is a very important part of the overall experience of sexual union. This activity is called afterplay, and it's so important that it even sets up the next sexual episode. You see, if she is fully satisfied, including the effects of afterplay, she'll begin the process of becoming aroused for the next time right away. But if she's left slightly dissatisfied because she didn't get any afterplay, that will delay her arousal for the next time. So, gentlemen, the next time you have sex, don't immediately roll over and go to sleep, or jump up and put on your pants. Instead, take a few moments to complete the sex act for your partner by engaging in some tender afterplay.

SIMULTANEOUS ORGASMS

I've mentioned some of the myths engendered by the entertainment industry, and here's another that I'd like to point out—terrific sex must include simultaneous orgasms. You've all seen the movies where both partners are groaning and moaning and then proceed to have their orgasms on cue, and after all, that's exactly what is happening. The director orders "orgasm" and the actors do as they're told. Here's a case where the porn world may actually be closer to the real world. Not that I've seen that many porn films, but since one of the features of most of them is the so-called "cum" shot, where the man is seen ejaculating outside the woman's vagina (or other orifice) in order to prove that what you are seeing is real, men and women in porn films don't necessarily have simultaneous orgasms. Well, readers, that's also true of most people.

I misspoke, or miswrote, in the paragraph when I seemed to say that simultaneous orgasms are a myth. It is certainly possible for two people to have their orgasms at the same time, and I would go further to say it is quite an enjoyable experience. The problem isn't with having simultaneous orgasms, but in trying to force yourselves to have them. If it works out, I say great, but if you're going to be disappointed because it didn't happen, then your expectations will end up spoiling the entire sexual episode for you, and that's not good.

EXPERIMENTATION

Case: Jan

My boyfriend and I have been going out for about a year and a half. We really love each other and hope to marry someday. The only problem is, our sex life is sort of boring. When we first started having sex, it was really great, but in the past few months, it seems that much of the spark has gone out of it, and we've been doing it a lot less. I'm afraid that if we do get married, we'll soon tire of sex altogether.

I get quite a number of letters like Jan's. You might think that it takes twenty years of marriage for a sex life to become boring, but it can happen a lot faster than that. In some instances it's really a symptom of a couple's relationship. If that's not going well, then you can understand that their sex life is not going to be in top form either. But it's not always a relationship issue. Sometimes the two people get into a sexual rut and boredom can set in no matter what their age, just as two people in their eighties may have a terrific sex life.

There's a saying, "If it ain't broke, don't try to fix it." If two people have sex using a certain pattern and both have orgasms ten times in a row, then they might have a tendency to do it the exact same way the next ten times, and the ten times after that. But picture, for a moment, your favorite food. Let's say it's steak. You might really enjoy a good steak dinner, but after fifty in a row, I'm sure you'd be sick of it. Or take your favorite CD. Sure you might enjoy playing it several times in a row, but how many times can you play it before you tire of it (or your roommate kills you)? So even though your favorite sex routine may work well for a time, you do have to add some variety to your sex life if you want to keep it vibrant.

Having just told you to add some variety, I now have to offer a caution or two. The first one is that you should never pressure anyone to do something they don't want to. You can ask them, but if you love them, at some point you have to stop asking, and you should never try to force them.

My other caution is not to push the envelope out too far. For example, some people decide that to add variety they need to add people. From what I've seen in my private practice, threesomes and so-called open marriages don't work. It's not the sex part that breaks down, but the emotional side. One person forms an attachment, or one person gets jealous, and then the entire relationship falls apart. So while I encourage you to experiment with different positions and different settings, try to stay within the boundaries of what your common sense tells you.

By the way, if it seems at all odd that the letter I chose is from a woman, it shouldn't be. You might assume that it's always the man who wants more sex and a greater variety than the woman, but that's a myth. I'm not saying there aren't many relationships in which it's the man who desires more variety, but there are also plenty of marriages where it is the woman who voices these complaints and it is the man who is stuck in a rut.

GAY SEX

Up to this point I've been speaking about heterosexual relationships, but just as in the real world, there are plenty of gay people on a college campus. While many college students appreciate leaving the pressures of parental supervision, gay students can be the ones who feel the most relief. If they haven't told their parents of their sexual orientation, then they may have been leading a double life, pretending to be heterosexual to their parents while either surreptitiously leading a gay lifestyle or hiding their true sexuality from everyone, perhaps including themselves.

College offers these individuals the freedom to be their true selves. Not every gay student who has been "in the closet" comes out as soon as they arrive, but once they see the gay organizations and meet other gay students, many do remove their heterosexual disguises and feel free, perhaps for the first time. This can lead to some sexual "bingeing," particularly among gay men, even if they do know the potential consequences. Perhaps it is because they haven't witnessed the deadly effects of AIDS by losing several friends that they feel they can be reckless. While I recognize the temptation to go overboard when faced with all this newfound freedom, having sex with multiple partners is just too dangerous and can cost you not only that very freedom but your life.

Because society still frowns on gay people, some young people try to push aside any attractions they may have for those of the same sex. Not only won't they admit to their parents and friends that they are gay, but they don't even admit it to themselves. But then when they are actually living with so many others of their own sex, they find themselves falling in love with someone of the same sex and have to face the reality of their sexual identity.

Make no mistake about it, this is not an easy thing to do, even in a new place full of strangers. Our society very much defines who we are by our sexual identity, and to suddenly make that switch can be a daunting task. Forgetting that at some point the person may have to face the people in their former lives, especially their parents, just to make that change within themselves can be very, very tough. My advice to anyone who is going through such a scenario is to get some professional help. On most college campuses there are counselors, some of whom are even familiar with this very predicament, or can recommend someone else who is. No one can make it an easy process, but the right advice can make it easier.

BI-SEX

Faced with so many choices, some young people are having sex with both the opposite sex and their own sex and calling themselves bisexuals. I'm not sure this term really exists. Oh, I'm not saying there aren't people living such a lifestyle, but I haven't seen any research that shows they are in fact bisexual. It's much more likely that they are either heterosexual, and are engaging in some homosexual activity because of peer pressure, or that they are really homosexuals who haven't completely admitted it to themselves or the world and so haven't made the switch to a completely homosexual lifestyle.

I know there are some celebrities, particularly some rock stars, who appear to be bisexual, but in my opinon I wouldn't play follow the leader with these people. Remember that their image is very important to their livelihood. Some may want to appear to be more "dangerous" than they really are and so pretend to be bisexual, while others may fear losing part of their audience if they admitted to being homosexual, and so they play at dating members of both sexes. Many people will occasionally wonder what it would be like to have sex with someone of their own sex, but such fantasies don't make them actually gay. The key to be being either heterosexual or homosexual is which type of person causes you to get aroused. If you can only get aroused by thinking of people of the same sex you are, then you are gay. But if this does not apply to you, then don't allow yourself to experiment just because it may be the fashionable thing to do.

SAFER SEX

I've mentioned condom use a few times as we've gone along, but I would be remiss not to give you more information about safer sex. Notice that I've used the word "safer" rather than safe. The only safe form of sex is masturbation. Any time that there are bodily fluids exchanged, there is some risk of catching a sexually transmitted disease, so while intercourse may be the most dangerous sexual activity, don't assume you are safe just because you're not at that stage of a relationship yet.

This is not a sex book, so I'm not going to go through the litany of sexually transmitted diseases (STDs), especially as I'm sure you were told all about them in high school. I want to make two points, however. One is that we still don't have a cure for AIDS. There are therapies that help people infected with HIV to live longer, but you should not assume that the threat posed by AIDS is any less. The other point applies particularly to women. There are several STDs that can make you infertile. With some you won't even feel any symptoms, but when the time comes for you to have a baby, you won't be able to. If some guy ever swears that he doesn't have AIDS, don't go around thinking that all of the other diseases can't affect you. Yes, doctors have treatments that can keep these diseases from killing you, but once you lose your ability to have children, you can never get it back.

Talking about STDs

The biggest obstacle to safer sex is awkwardness. People feel awkward talking about sexual matters, and by not communicating honestly with each other, they put themselves at risk. Therefore, if you want to protect yourself from catching a sexually transmitted disease, you must confront those feelings of awkwardness and say what needs to be said to maintain your own safety. But, of course, it is a lot easier to say this in a book than to actually say the words to a potential sex partner.

The Benefits of Condom Use

The way to truly protect yourself is to only have sex with healthy people. And the only way to tell if someone is not carrying a sexually transmitted disease is if they are tested. But if you're still dealing with the issue of whether you're going to have sex together, how easy is it going to be to ask the other person to get themselves tested, and then wait for the results? And then hope that while this other person is waiting around, they don't have sex with somebody else and catch a disease they didn't have before? I know I can talk about testing till I'm blue in the face and the majority of couples are not going to be tested before they become sexually active. But anybody, of either sex, can go into a drugstore and purchase some condoms, and then insist that they be used.

Condoms do not offer 100 percent protection against either pregnancy or STDs. They can break. They can slip off. They can be forgotten to be used. But if you're really a stickler for using condoms and are careful to use them the right way, they can offer you a great deal of protection. Would it be better if you only had sex with people who were tested and so proved they had a clean bill of health? Obviously, but in the real world, that's not always going to happen, so make sure you have some condoms handy.

Most men don't like to use condoms. They say it lessens their pleasure. That may be so, but a woman who is on the pill is not protected against STDs. If the man insists on not using condoms, then the woman must insist that he be tested, and she must have the confidence in her man that he won't have sex with anyone else after he's been tested.

How Safe Is Oral Sex

Many young people ask me about the safety of oral sex. From what I can gather, there is less of a risk that you will catch an STD, and AIDS in particular, through oral sex than intercourse. *But that risk is not zero.* You can protect yourself against an unintended pregnancy by engaging only in oral sex, but you are not practicing safe sex, or even *safer* sex. So don't look at oral sex as a means of protecting yourself against anything but an unintended pregnancy. If you're both virgins, then the risks of having an STD are probably small, but if one of the pair is more experienced, oral sex is not the answer to protecting yourself.

ON REMAINING A VIRGIN

There are groups who are pushing for young people to abstain from having sex until they are married. That's a traditional value and was a very good one in the days when people got married at an early age and there was no way to prevent an unintended pregnancy. Today we expect our young people to put marriage off until they finish college, at least, and many until they've got their career off the ground. Is it likely that all young people will remain virgins until they're in the mid-twenties? I don't think so, which is why I do my best to instruct people how to have sex without getting pregnant or catching a disease.

But what if you do decide to remain a virgin? Or even if you didn't plan on it but there you are, ready to graduate college and still not having had sexual intercourse with anyone? Is that so terrible? Is it something you should be ashamed of? Should you have slept with that guy or girl at that party when you were both drunk? Does being a virgin really make a difference in the type of person you are?

There was a time when an adulteress was made to wear a scarlet A on her clothing so that everyone would know the sin she committed. But nobody has to know whether you are a virgin. Your time will come, just be a little patient. When you look back on your life, having remained a virgin through college will probably be only a blip.

On the other hand, if you're not only a virgin, but someone who never had a significant other and feels lonely and badly about it, then that's another story. There could be many reasons for that, and I can't go into them all in this particular book, but I will say that those feelings are something you should address, and as soon as possible. I would suggest that you go for some sort of counseling. Why do I say that? Not because I think you're crazy, but because I think you could be helped. If you had a toothache and I advised you to go to a dentist, would you hold it against me? Of course not. Well, if your heart aches, for whatever reason, and there is help available, is it any less valid a reason to seek out help? I think not. I'm not suggesting that you go to lifelong psychotherapy. All I'm saying is that you should seek out a counselor, tell him or her your problem, and see what type of advice you receive. If it seems logical and doable, then go ahead and follow it. If it can help you solve this particular problem, I think you'll agree that it was worth your time and money.

8

YOU WILL GO HOME AGAIN

How Not to Regret It

When your parents dropped you off at college for the first time, it was a very/moderately/slightly traumatic experience to watch them drive away. But most of you probably adapted fairly quickly to college life, and soon your dorm room began to feel like home. Depending on how far away your college is from your hometown, your first visit back might not occur until Thanksgiving, which is a short period and usually spent with family. But as the years fly by, there will be plenty of other breaks, including the long summer vacations.

You've probably heard the expression "You can't go home again." While it doesn't absolutely apply to a returning college student, there are going to be changes in your relationships back home that you should be aware of. And I don't want to alarm you, because they won't all be bad, but life as you knew it will never be exactly the same.

YOUR ROOM

Let's start with the basics, your room. Whether or not you shared your room with a sibling, when you return you're going to find changes, and as time goes on, there'll be more and more of them. Please don't take this personally. Unless your parents occupy a fifty-room mansion, all families need extra space. Nature abhors a vacuum, so if there's any empty space lying about, it's going to be filled. When you and your belongings left for college, a vacuum was formed in your room and so your family was irresistibly pulled into filling it.

Now some college students actually do lose their room. A younger sister or brother takes over the space entirely, and when the college student returns, they're assigned a new place. This may seem unfair, but after all, if your room is nicer and you're not occupying it three-quarters of the time, why should it remain vacant? But even if you had a room of your own and nobody moved in, the odds of it remaining precisely as you left it are slim. First of all, your parents, and more likely your mother, may have been making plans for the room long before you packed up your things. Maybe she put off a much needed paint job, knowing that it would be a less confusing process if you were out of the way. Or maybe she had personal designs for it, such as making it into a study or room in which she could pursue a hobby that required her to spread out a bit and leave things lying around. Anyway, as I said, though you might not have been aware of it, your room may have been targeted for changes months before your departure. Now while you were at college, your mental image of your room remained the same. And if you were at all unhappy with dorm living, thoughts of getting back to it gave you some comfort. Obviously to return and find it not looking at all as you left it (which is guaranteed since all your favorite things are still at school) is going to be a shock.

THE NEW YOU

Just as you pictured your room unchanged all those months you were away, your parents continued to picture you exactly as you were before you left. And so just as you may be left a bit rocky by the changes in your room, they're going to be slightly shocked at the changes in you.

While your room may undergo physical changes that are apparent to all, the growth process that you'll undergo in college won't be (unless you're one of those who puts on those "freshman 15" pounds). In fact, you won't even notice it all that much, until your parents' expectations clash with the new you, because even though your parents sent you off to college in order that you would learn and grow, part of them still wants you to remain their baby. You've certainly noted that conflict while you were living at home, but the process of growth and compromise had been a gradual one that had become a natural fit. (Or you were constantly fighting like cats and dogs, in which case the conflicts that arise when you go back home will feel "normal.") But when you return home, it will be a little like trying to fit into a pair of jeans several months after you'd gone through a growth spurt. Maybe with a little effort you can close the zipper, but there's nothing you can do about the fact that the legs no longer cover your ankles.

While living on your own, you will have learned to treasure your new independence. In college you can go to bed whenever you want and, apart from class schedules, get up whenever you want. You can leave your room messy. You can eat what you select. You can stay on the phone as long as you like (or at least as long as you can afford). Friends can drop in on you and you can drop in on them. And if you have a boyfriend or girlfriend, what you do together is nobody else's business. When you return home, each of these issues, along with many others, can be a major source of conflict.

> **Q.** I always used to look forward to Christmas vacation when I was in high school, but when I went home from college for a month, it felt like I was going to prison. At school I almost never go to bed before 2 A.M., and some nights it's not until morning. My parents demanded that I tell them exactly when I'd be coming home, and where I was going. My room at school is a mess and I like it that way. Back home, my mom started screaming right away about the pile of clothes. And at college there's always loud music playing, but that also gave my parents a fit, especially at night if I had friends over. How do I get them to stop treating me like a little kid when I come home?

> **A.** What you have to understand is that college isn't the real world. It's an artificial environment that allows you

more freedom than you'll ever have at any other time in your life. While it's great to take advantage of it, when you go home, you're actually going back into the real world. Your parents need peace and quiet at night because they have to go to work the next morning, to earn the money to pay for all that freedom you have at college. So don't think that they are merely treating you as a little kid. They're trying to survive their work lives, and maybe they're under a lot of pressure, which the holidays can make even worse. So instead of selfishly thinking of yourself, try to be a little bit more considerate of their needs. After all, you'll be going back to college soon enough, while they'll still be toiling away.

If you go home thinking that now you're a grownup and should be treated like one, then you're going to have to act like one. The more you prove to your parents that you have become more mature, the easier it is going to be to resolve these conflicts. But if you insist on returning to your childlike ways, then you're going to be treated like a child, and that can lead to some major fights.

Here's a simple example: laundry. When you're at school, you're responsible for keeping your clothes clean, and whether you do a good job or go around wearing dirty clothes, it's up to you. But if, when you come home, all you bring back are dirty clothes that you dump in the usual place, expecting your parents to wash them for you, then you are not acting like an adult. You are reverting to your childlike ways. By exhibiting these childish behaviors, you are basically telling your parents you haven't really changed, and that gives them permission to continue to treat you the way they did before you left. But if you continue to maintain responsibility for your clothes, doing your own laundry, then you're saying loud and clear, I've grown up and you have to treat me differently.

I used laundry as an example, but there are lots of ways you can give this same message, and the more of them you adopt, the more you'll be accepted as a grown-up.

TIPS

- Don't just eat dinner, help to shop and prepare it. And that goes for breakfast and lunch too, especially if you're on vacation while your parents are still working.

- If you have younger siblings who need a ride or help with homework, don't wait to be asked. Volunteer to provide these services (and spend some quality time with them).

- Consider using headphones when listening to music. Your parents may have gotten used to some peace and quiet.

- Don't go rushing out to see your friends the first night you're back. Put aside some time to let your parents know how college is treating you and to catch up on their news.

If they see you exhibiting traits that prove you've matured by being on your own, then you have every right to expect them to treat you as a more mature person. For example, if you don't have a curfew at college, you shouldn't have one at home either. However, as this new, more mature person, you also have to show your parents that you still love them and respect their feelings, so while it may be all right to walk in with the dawn, they have to be sure you are safe. That means letting them know, at least vaguely, where you are going, and if you decide to stay out a lot later than you originally planned, giving them a phone call. You'd be surprised how much peace of mind that will give them, and how much it can lessen conflicts. Walking out the door saying "Later" is not acceptable behavior. In fact, I bet you don't do that to your roommates. In case you get a phone call, you want them to know that you're in class or at a hockey game. So don't treat your parents worse just because they used to control you. If you really are an adult, then you'll understand that telling them where you're going and when you'll be back doesn't mean you need their permission, but is just good manners. Teens need to revolt to show their growing independence, but adults are past that stage, so if you want to be treated as an adult, you have to act like one.

However, because you are still living in their house, no matter how much like an adult you may feel and they may wish to treat you, there are going to be some limits that you are not going to be able to go beyond. These limits will be set at different levels in each household, but I'll mention a few that generally will hold true in every home.

ALCOHOL USE

While your parents may even enjoy being able to share a drink with you, and will offer you a glass if they're imbibing, you have to be more careful about overindulging. In the first place, you're more likely to be using a car when visiting friends at home than you would at school, and so it is just more dangerous. But while your friends at school may think it funny to see you stagger into your room, your parents will take a very different attitude. If you do go out drinking with your friends, make sure there is a designated driver, and give yourself enough time to overcome most of the effects of the last round before walking through the front (or back) door.

BOYFRIENDS AND GIRLFRIENDS

While you'll be delighted to give up the teachers and their assignments when you're home on vacation, you might find it harder to separate yourself from a boyfriend or girlfriend you had on campus and saw every day. Unless you both come from the same hometown, you might invite your boyfriend or girlfriend home with you. This may cause overnight visits, which are almost always a source of conflict. In the first place, since your family sent away only one person, who is rather special to them, they're going to have somewhat of a problem adjusting to having two people come back. If they've missed you, they're going to want to have you all to themselves for a while, and having to share their "baby" is going to be difficult. There are also going to be issues of privacy. The household family dynamics will have changed just by the fact that you weren't there, and the adjustment process will be even more difficult if there's a new person added to the mix. And, of course, there's the issue of sex.

Many students who've been sexually active while away at school expect that scenario to continue when they return home. While I'm not saying that you won't find opportunities to have sex, spending the night in the same bed probably won't be one of them. Now there are some liberal parents who don't mind that their children have someone of the opposite sex share their bed, but a great many will balk at the idea. Since it is their house, you have to respect their position. If the relationship lasts, after a time they may change their mind on this issue. And by time, I'm speaking years here, not days. But then again they may not.

If you don't understand that, let me offer you an example that I think will help you. What are your feelings when you think of your parents having sex? If you're like most people, it's a subject you don't want to contemplate. Since you don't have kids of your own, you can't see what it's like to think of the opposite end of that spectrum, but if you consider your feelings about your parents having sex, I think you can be a little more understanding of their feelings about you being sexually active. It's not that they may not realize that you and your significant other are having sex at college, but you have to admit that it is more difficult to accept if it's happening under their own roof. Again, if two people want to have sex, they're going to find a way. If both your parents work during the day, then your problem is immediately solved. And so even if you had no intention of actually engaging in sex while your parents are in the next room, expect that your parents are going to want the two of you to have different official sleeping quarters. (Whether there is some unofficial sneaking around during the night is another story, and may be more tolerated as long as both beds are occupied in the morning.)

Is this attitude a little hypocritical? Yes. But again, think back on your attitude toward your parents. Unless they had a bad marriage, they were definitely having sex all those years you were living at home. But for the most part, I'm sure they kept their sex lives private. All I'm suggesting is that you show them the same respect they showed you. And when you get married and have children of your own, you'll go through the same cycle.

TIPS

- Never surprise your parents with a guest, particularly a boyfriend or girlfriend. Make sure you discuss such a visit ahead of time.

- If your parents don't say anything specifically about sleeping arrangements, assume that they are going to be separate. That way you won't be disappointed and start an embarrassing argument in front of your boyfriend or girlfriend.

- If you're the one who is visiting, make sure you put on your very best manners. Initially there may be some antagonism when you arrive, and you can ward off most of it by being super-polite.

WHO GOES WHERE DURING THE HOLIDAYS

Once you start dating, there's going to be a source of conflict that may never be resolved: where to spend the holidays. If the two families involved, yours and your friend's, live so far apart that going back and forth on the same day, or even the next day, is not possible, some people are going to wind up feeling disappointed.

Given such factors as the distance between the families, their religions, the size of the families, your birth order, etc., there are too many possible permutations for me to give too much direct advice. Each case has to stand on its own merits. But I can give you some general advice on how to handle these situations.

First of all, make sure you are very specific with everyone—your boyfriend or girlfriend, your family, and your friends. It's easy to dawdle, not making any decisions, keeping everything up in the air. That's a mistake. It allows everyone's hopes to go up, or expectations to stay the same, and the closer to the specific holiday someone finds out they're going to be disappointed, the worse their feelings are going to be. They will have spent more time imagining what the holiday is going to be like with you around, they may well have talked about it with all their friends, and so they'll be even more disappointed when you drop your bombshell announcement. If the problem is unavoidable, the earlier you face up to it, the better. Yes, it may mean that you're going to hear more complaints and for a longer period of time, but since you're the cause of their discomfort, you have to be willing to take some abuse. It will make them feel a little bit better and it's part of the price you have to pay.

I would also advise you to play Solomon and weigh your decision carefully. Just because you're in love doesn't give you the right to hurt anybody. The better course may be for you and your boyfriend or girlfriend to spend the holidays with your families and away from each other. Whatever you do, don't put any pressure on the other person to be with you. Be generous and make sure to offer that they go to be with their family and that you understand, even if your heart is breaking. If you were married, that would be another story. Then you could alternate as there would be a definite future ahead of you. But a boyfriend or girlfriend does not come ahead of family.

And remember, as much as the two of you want to be together for that particular holiday, on the specific day, the person who is away from his or her family is going to feel blue. That person has a long history of spending that holiday with their family. Often members of an extended family are also there. So while it might seem romantic to be together, the day itself may turn out to be a bit of a disappointment. That's why you shouldn't just jump at the chance to let one family fall by the wayside but should only do it if the circumstances really merit it. After all, once school starts again, you'll be back together and your families won't be seeing you for months.

SIBLINGS

There's no doubt that your parents missed you while you were away. Although younger siblings may not show their emotions so openly, I can guarantee that they too felt your absence. Even if you normally fight constantly, they will miss even that. After all, it's a form of attention that will have been missing while you were away. You may have been too busy to spend much time thinking of them, but every time they passed your room or saw that empty chair at the dinner table, they thought of you.

And by the way, while you were growing up at college, they were doing some growing too. For one thing, they undoubtedly had to assume responsibilities that were yours, such as taking out the garbage or taking care of a family pet. So, young people change constantly, and just as your parents will notice the changes that occurred in you over a period of months, you'll notice some changes in your siblings.

In one manner this gives you an opportunity for a new beginning in your relationship with your siblings. Sure it will be great fooling around with them the way you always used to do, but also try to talk to them as you would to an adult. They'll have a different perspective on how the family survived without you, and they may have problems they'll want to ask your advice about.

What happens to most sisters and brothers as they become adults is that they become more like good friends. The complete maturation of the relationship won't happen until you are all adults, but the process definitely began when you left for college and you should encourage its growth.

TIPS

- Spend some quality time, one on one, with each of your siblings. Go out for pizza, or just for a walk or bike ride. If you're away from your parents, your sibling will be able to talk more openly and it will give you a chance to do the same.

- If it's appropriate, offer your siblings the opportunity to visit you on campus. It's an experience you'll both enjoy and it will give them a better picture of what college life is all about.

- If you're going to be away for any or all of your siblings' birthdays, try to do something special for them while you are around.

FRIENDS

While you may have sworn to be best-friends-for-life at your high school graduation, there are no guarantees that those promises will hold. If you ask the adults you know how many friends they still see from high school, you'll find that they are few and far between. High school is a special time, and while you are there, you really are very close to your friends, but once you are separated, without the blood ties that family members have, it can be difficult to maintain that friendship.

While you were in high school, you were all sharing the same classes and had basically the same goal—to get into college. But once you're in college, you all start taking separate paths, in terms of both personal relationships and careers. Just in choosing your college you already experienced the first beginnings of separation. Most of you didn't choose a college because someone else was going there. You chose what you thought was the right college for you. That process has to continue, and as you make those choices, you end up separating from your high school classmates. You learn that there aren't enough hours in the day to do all you have to do and maintain close ties to high school friends.

Those changes may not be immediately apparent. The first time you return home for a break, you'll definitely gravitate toward these old buddies. But as you all start to grow and mature, you'll develop new friends, first in college, then in your work life, as well as start families, and so those relationships will begin to fade.

Now this won't be true for everybody. There's a large element of chance to all of this. There are people who are very close to some high school friends. In fact there are people close to their old grammar school friends, because their paths kept them together, and perhaps because they planned it that way or because that's just the way things turned out. I'm not saying there's anything wrong with keeping your old friends. All I'm saying is that the forces pulling you apart will likely be stronger than those that could keep you together, and so it shouldn't come as a total surprise if you start to drift apart. And if it allows you to grow in the best direction for you, then this separation won't be such a bad thing.

OLD FLAMES

The one type of friendship that can be most awkward to keep is with an old boyfriend or girlfriend. Assuming that neither of you has found someone new at college, then you'll be getting back together during the breaks. But in many cases you're going to find that the relationship is somehow just not the same. Again, some people end up marrying their high school sweetheart, even if they don't go to the same college, and if that happens, great. Those people don't need my advice. But it's a much trickier situation to handle an old flame when it starts to die out.

Any two former members of a couple who haven't seen each other for a while are going to be very nervous when they get back together for the first time. Even if they've been communicating regularly, there'll be a part of them that wonders if their love is still what it used to be. And you know what? There's no real way of telling until you actually spend some time together.

LOVE HAS A NASTY HABIT OF DISAPPEARING OVERNIGHT

Those are lyrics from a Beatles tune, "I'm Looking Through You." More of the song goes: "I'm looking through you. Where did you go? I thought I knew you. What did I know? You don't look different but you have changed. I'm looking through you, you're not the same."

Though songwriters may be dipping into personal relationships for their inspiration, if they have broad appeal it's because they're touching on emotions with universal qualities. And you may end up going through one of these all too human experiences, the end of a relationship.

> **Q.** My girlfriend and I were together for my last two years in high school. She was a junior so she stayed in the same school while I went away to college. She's applying to colleges now and she wants to go to the same one I do. While we still see each other when I'm home, because I don't

want to hurt her, I don't want her coming to my college. I don't have a girlfriend there, per se, but there are some women I've dated, though I didn't tell my girlfriend. She's really sweet and all, but my tastes have changed, and I guess we're not really meant to be. How do I get her not to apply to my school without breaking up with her?

A. You can't, and if you're not in love with her, you should tell her. Obviously she's waiting for you, and wants to go to college with you. At some point you're going to tell her you don't love her anymore, and she's going to feel that pain anyway. But she's going to feel even worse because she's going to think what a fool she was to wait for you all that time. So rather than delay breaking this sad news to her, do it as soon as possible. Then you won't have to worry about her applying to your college, because it will be the last place on earth she'd want to go.

When an active relationship falls apart, it's often volcanic in nature as the fights between the former lovers grow to the point where they can't stand each other. But when two people are apart for a long period, the flame can just die out on its own. If both halves of the former couple experience this at the same time, then the parting can be relatively painless. What's sad is when one person falls out of love and the other doesn't.

Breakups are almost always painful, and so there is going to be some pressure to avoid them. Some of that pressure is going to come from your friends and parents. They'll all expect the two of you to still be a couple, and if you don't have a particular reason for breaking up, they'll do all they can to prevent it. Holidays will be another influence on maintaining at least a semblance that you're still a couple. Bad news is always to be avoided at these times of forced gaiety. And then there's the fact that you'll be going away again soon, which makes it easy to put off.

While I don't want to put any pressure on you to break up, I would encourage you to do some hard thinking about your relationship if it seems to have become a pale shadow of its former self. That probably means you might start actively looking for someone to date when you get back to school, and if you leave home as part of a couple, then you'll really be cheating. And what if your friend's feelings haven't changed? Your friend will be waiting patiently for you while you go off in another direction. You owe it to him or her to have an honest discussion. Even if you're not ready to completely break off the relationship, you could give each other permission to date. As you've seen, I'm all for white lies, but that's when they are protecting someone from being hurt needlessly. In a case like this, to hide your doubts may have the opposite effect. So don't just take the easy way out, but choose the most honorable path.

TIPS

- Usually the hardest part of such conversations is getting them started. If you're lucky, there may be a movie out about a relationship that you can go to see together, and that will allow the conversation to steer itself in the direction of analyzing your relationship immediately afterward. If there isn't the right kind of movie out, see if one is available at your video store and make a point of watching it together, even if you've already seen it.

- Giving an advance warning of your feelings can help to ease the way. If you call up your friend and say "Let's get together later, I think we need to talk," you'll be giving them a message that there's something serious you want to discuss. By doing that, when you do announce your news, it won't be so much of a shock.

- If worse comes to worse and you can't bring yourself to talk about your relationship while you are together, then definitely drop your friend a line or e-mail as soon as you get back to college. Writing is easier, and it does accomplish the same purpose, but be prepared for a phone call that might not be so painless.

Of course the tables might be turned on you, and instead of being the one to announce the end of the relationship, you're on the receiving end of this news. When two people are seeing each other regularly, it's likely there have been signs that they've been drifting apart. Even if they didn't want to acknowledge the signs, they will have subconsciously registered them. But if you haven't seen each other in several months, and if your own feelings haven't changed at all, then being told that the relationship is on the rocks, or even finished, can be devastating.

In life, there is no way to completely avoid pain. And emotional pain that stems from a loss, be that through the death of a person or the end of a long-lasting relationship, can be the most painful of all. Dealing with the end of a relationship is very similar to coping with the death of a loved one. There has to be a period of mourning, where you allow yourself to be sad. Don't try to forget the other person, or the things you did together, because you can't forget. Eventually the pain will subside, and you will be able to move on.

Even though you can't rush this process, you shouldn't try to cling to your sadness either. Don't purposefully watch sad movies, but after some time has passed, seek out comedies. If there's a song that makes you want to cry, take it out of your play rotation. If there's an outfit that reminds you of the other person, put it away. While it's perfectly okay to be miserable, you needn't wallow in it forever. The good thing about being back at college is that there won't be any reminders of your boyfriend or girlfriend. Hopefully you can get over this relationship before you have to go back home where some reminders will be unavoidable.

YOUR RELATIVES

There's another group of people you'll be seeing when you go home: your relatives. Even if you don't see all of them regularly, you're likely to see at least some of them because of the holidays.

My first piece of advice regarding relatives you're about to see concerns what may have happened to them in the interim. While you were away, there may have been a death or birth or wedding that you should make mention of when you first greet them. Before the family get-together starts, make sure to ask your parents to clue you in on any important news so that you won't wind up with egg on your face. And having this information, don't forget to use it, by saying to the person either "Sorry about your loss" or "Congratulations on. . . ." Even if the event took place a couple of months ago, any adult will expect to hear this type of acknowledgment of what took place.

One of the biggest problems a returning college student faces with such visits is that everyone you see is going to ask you the same question, "How's college?" After a while you're going to get tired of repeating the same answer. What's the solution to this? It's not just to say "Fine." Instead you have to give each of them a different answer.

I give lots of lectures every year, literally all over the world. The people who book these lectures often ask for a description of what I'm going to say. At the very least they're looking for a specific title. But I always insist that the title be generic, like "An Evening with Dr. Ruth," because I don't go in with a prepared speech. If I kept giving the same speech over and over again, I'd be bored to tears and couldn't be an effective speaker. In order for me to hold my own attention, I need to improvise. I need to be thinking on my feet. Now sure I have certain classic stories, some of which I always manage to weave in. But I'm just as likely to talk about something that happened to me last week, or even a few minutes before I got on stage. And that's exactly what you have to learn to do.

You've been gone for a few months. Lots of things have happened to you while you were away, but you can't tell your grandmother or Aunt Alice about every incident. And certainly some of the things that happened to you were more interesting than others. So my suggestion is to give each person a different story. If one of these stories gets a particularly good reaction, then you might repeat that one more often, but don't let it dominate your repertoire, because if you get bored telling it, then that will begin to show in the conversation.

But suppose you say to me: "Dr. Ruth, nothing very exciting happened. There's nothing I can say. Or at least nothing I can repeat to my family." If that's what you feel like saying to me after reading the last paragraph, then you have to do something about that. Probably it's not true and you're just being lazy. Maybe you don't care that much about Aunt Alice, so you don't feel like racking your brains in order to entertain her. I don't even know your Aunt Alice, who might be the world's biggest bore, but that is a terrible attitude. You see, the reason it's a terrible attitude is because of how it affects you. Just because the person you're talking to is boring doesn't mean that you have to be bored. You can entertain yourself. But to do that is an art that you can only learn by practicing it, so instead of looking at Aunt Alice's question as a waste of your time, look at it as an opportunity to refine your skills at conversation.

You want a specific suggestion? Here's one. At the end of every semester most college students have some papers due, so it's likely that you just finished writing one a few days earlier. It doesn't matter what the topic was; just say, "I just wrote a paper on such and such and discovered such and such." I'm sure there will have been at least one new thing you learned in writing your paper. That should be enough to trigger a discussion for at least a few minutes. Uncle Henry comes along next. Tell him that you just took a math final. That will trigger another discussion, and that will go in a different direction. Next comes your grandmother and you'll tell her about some club you joined. And your cousin? Bring up the food in the cafeteria.

You see, these people aren't looking for a specific answer from you, so you can talk freely about anything that happened and they'll be pleased. They're interested in what happens to you, because they are your relatives and have watched you grow up, but they're also looking to make conversation. When they ask you a question, it's as if someone serves the ball to you in a game of tennis. It's up to you to hit it back to them, but there's no particular place you have to hit it. All you have to do is get it back over the net.

Case: Frank

Frank went to Columbia University and joined a fraternity. The fraternity house was a brownstone building that faced a typical New York side street. One winter's day a homeless person wandered in, probably to use the bathroom first, but then he sort of made himself at home and stayed for a couple of days. The fraternity brothers allowed him to hang around, both because it was sort of a good deed, as it was bitterly cold outside, and because the experience was amusing.

To actually hear Frank, who is a wonderful raconteur, tell the story is hilarious. Why am I bringing this up? Because such events happen to everyone, but not everyone takes full advantage of them. Certainly weeks can go by when the word of the day is dull, but every once in a while you'll see or experience something interesting. That you should be working to maximize the number of those days is another matter, but for now I want you to spend a little time recalling the stories you already have, and prepare yourself for new ones that will come along. Try to remember the details that will make the stories work in conversation. And don't be afraid to elaborate a little. If you're talking to someone, you're not being a historian but rather an entertainer. If changing a few details makes the story funnier or more interesting, then go ahead and take some liberties with the truth. They'll be glad you did, and so will you.

I might also recommend keeping a diary or journal. At some point you're going to want to remember what occurred during your college years, and it will be a lot of fun going back to read the various happenings, even the everyday ones. You'll read a certain professor's name, whom you have completely forgotten, and a whole flood of memories will come back to you. By the way, this doesn't have to be a formal book with the word diary on it. It could be a simple notebook. Or a document on your computer. I don't keep a diary, per se, but I do have lots of notes in my appointment book, which by the end of the year is twice its original size. Going through these books helps me remember what I did during that year.

9

BREAKING OUT INTO THE WORLD
WIDE WORLD

The original purpose of a higher education was purely a pursuit of learning. While learning for the sake of improving one's mind is still a component of today's college curriculum, for most students it's not the main incentive for spending as much as $35,000 a year to attend college. Instead, a college degree is looked at as a stepping-stone toward earning a living, which, while necessary, is a little sad.

To have a successful career these days requires more education because there is so much more to learn. For most of human history, it was possible for an educated person to know almost everything there was to know. Now an individual can't even come close to it in a lifetime, much less in four years. There is so much more information already available, and so much new information created every day, that there is no place in our brains to cram it all in. You can get a liberal arts degree that will give you a healthy smattering of our culture, but we, as a society, now know too much to pass on all of it to any one individual. In fact, we now know so much within each discipline that it becomes difficult to master even one area, leaving even less room to learn about everything else.

So now reality has bumped squarely head on with the esoteric, and most students today are studying with the aim of getting a job, rather than to turn themselves into more fully developed intellectual human beings. This saddens me because I know that once a college student has graduated, the likelihood of their education being resumed, beyond taking courses even more exclusively in some specialty, is very small. So we will end up having fewer and fewer people who look at life from a global perspective. People won't have either the time or the inclination to listen to an Italian opera or attend a concert of Mozart's music or go to an exhibition of Marc Chagall's work at a fine arts museum or sit enthralled in a theater watching a drama by Anton Chekov unfold. And the most important reason they'll ignore these cultural masterpieces is that they'll never have been exposed to them and so won't appreciate their worth. So my advice to you is to take advantage of your college years to broaden yourself as much as possible.

That said, let me go on to the subject of this chapter, which is to help you advance your way toward a profitable career.

APHORISMS

On the off chance you don't know the meaning of the word "aphorism," let me offer a couple:

Strike while the iron is hot.

The early bird catches the worm.

That's right, an aphorism is one of those old sayings. But you know what? Some of those old sayings carry a lot of truth in them and are very applicable to the subject at hand—discovering a career path that will maximize your well-being. Notice I didn't say fatten your bank account, because while money is important, and if you have to work, you might as well make the most money you can, but how much you are paid isn't the only ingredient to a satisfying work life. If you hate your job, the pay becomes secondary.

Now some people are able to decide well in advance what their career is going to be and they work very hard to get there. Medical students certainly come to mind, and in some fields, like medicine, you do need to have a one-track mind or you will never reach your destination. You must begin taking science courses in high school and stick to it right through college, because there is so much science that you have to learn that you can never catch up if you don't get an early start. On the other hand, if you want to become a lawyer, you can major in almost anything as an undergraduate and still get into law school, just as long as you get good grades and do well on the LSAT.

Most careers fall somewhere between these two extremes. In other words, for you to follow a particular career path, there are one or two majors from which you should choose, and then take the courses required to fulfill that major. College students often find themselves in a bind, however, because they don't exactly know what it is they want to be "when they grow up." After all, if you've never worked at a job, how are you going to know whether you like it? And if you've spent four years training, and then it turns out you can't stand it, what do you do then? In real life there is no punting option.

A STITCH IN TIME SAVES NINE

In order not to find yourself in the above situation, what you should do is to find some work in that particular field. It won't be exactly what you plan on doing, as most employers don't give much responsibility to college students working part-time or during the summer, but it should give you enough of a taste that you can tell whether it is a career in which you could be happy.

In order to get this "stitch," that is, some time working in a field you are considering, you might have to become a slave, which in business parlance is called an internship. Most colleges allow their students to get credit for working at a job in their field. (In some cases, you must do an internship to fulfill the requirements.) So, for example, if you are a communications major, you will receive credit for being an intern at a public relations or advertising agency.

Will such an internship be particularly interesting? Probably not. You'll be asked to do all sorts of menial tasks that the paid employees don't like to do. However, while many firms do take advantage of their interns in this way, they usually also give them a taste of what a real job would be like. There is someone of whom you can ask questions and who might even let you handle some important duties. How much worthwhile experience you get is somewhat up to you.

Whether or not you take any course in psychology, there are general attributes of human psychology that you must be aware of and make use of too. For example, most employers who use interns feel somewhat guilty at having people work for them for nothing. So if an intern asks for something reasonable, like being allowed to attend a press conference they've been helping the firm put together, they'll probably get a positive response.

But to get such treatment, you also have to show yourself off in the best light. Even if you're assigned to the mailroom where the employees can wear jeans, you should dress somewhat nicer and do whatever it takes to make a good impression. Besides getting a chance to look more closely at the job, an intern who makes a very good impression may even land a paid position after graduation, but to do that you're going to have to show some initiative.

Since interns usually don't get paid beyond some expense money for travel, employers have no choice but to cut them some slack. It's then easy for an intern to fall into the trap of doing the least possible work. I say trap, because while it may appear that the intern is getting away with something, they are in fact hurting themselves. The intern's supervisor is not going to think very highly of this person, and so any chance of getting a job will evaporate. And the intern also won't learn as much as he or she could from the experience, so that it can turn out to be a total waste of time.

TIPS

- You may not be the only intern, so it's your job to stand out by working harder and showing more initiative. Dressing up may also help you.

- Sometimes there's a period when there is little to do for an intern. Even if you are just sitting there twiddling your thumbs, you must always be on the alert to volunteer should any opportunity come along to do a useful task.

- If there are other interns and they are more interested in having a good time than working, try not to join them. It may be tempting to be one of the guys or gals but it's not worth it if it negates the value of your internship.

What happens if, as a result of your internship, you decide that you hate the field you chose for yourself? The first thing you have to do is examine the situation to make sure it wasn't something about the particular place where you worked rather than the field itself. But if you decide that you're not cut out to be a ——, then you have to think of that internship as one of the most valuable experiences of your life. Just imagine if you hadn't been an intern and you had gone ahead with your plans to enter that field and, only after having invested a good deal of your time and energy, then discovered the truth. You would really have been up the creek. But thanks to your internship, you now have a second chance to decide what you want to be, and because those don't come around that often, that's worth a lot.

But what if you're about to enter your senior year and now you want to change majors? Is it too late? Are you locked into pursuing this career even if you hate it? The answer is no, from both the psychological point of view and the practical one. It should be obvious that if you discover you hate a particular profession you shouldn't follow through, even if it means changing your major. And from the practical point of view, perhaps you'll have to go to summer school to finish the requirements, but that should not present a major obstacle. After all, you're setting yourself on a course that could last fifty years, so if it takes a few months to navigate yourself in the right direction, it's well worth the effort.

TIPS

- If you're having difficulty choosing between two career paths that require different majors, consider taking a dual major. Even if you don't end up completing both, it will give you the opportunity to choose right up to the last minute without worrying about having to suddenly play catch-up because you're short some credits.

By the way, if you do change majors, don't think that you're alone in having made a mistake choosing your first major. Studies have shown that almost half of all college graduates now feel that they should have chosen another major, so if you manage to make a switch, the likelihood is that you'll be doing yourself a favor.

PAYING THE PIPER

Not everyone can afford to take an internship. Many students have to work for pay while they're in college in order to meet their educational expenses, and if that's the case, how much the job pays may matter more than what it entails. But while you may not have much choice in your first part-time job, perhaps because your school will assign you where they need you or because you don't know the lay of the land when you first arrive, I would suggest that you do some research to see what other positions may be available, either at your college or in nearby towns. Be on the lookout for jobs that would offer you both financial remuneration and experience related to what you want to do in life. Put your best efforts into this job search, for it may pay off handsomely in unexpected ways.

TIPS

- Try to make friends with the staff in your college placement office. They're the first to know about jobs that are going to be posted, and if they like you, and know what type of work you're looking for, they might be able to tip you off when the right opportunity comes along.

- While the ideal job may not be located in the town your college is in, companies located not too far away could be a source of employment in your field, so do some research using the yellow pages or the Internet.

- During the spring semester, talk to seniors about their jobs. They won't be around next fall, so you'll get a head start by applying for a job for the next year.

THE SQUEAKY WHEEL GETS THE OIL

If you want something, no matter what it is, you have to ask for it. Now if you walk into a candy store with a dollar in your pocket and you ask for a bar of chocolate, you're 100 percent sure of getting what you ask for. But if you want a certain type of job, and you're not sure which companies might be hiring and a lot of other people are looking for the same type of job, then the odds of your getting that job lessen considerably. So how do you increase those odds? By squeaking as loud and as often as you can.

While there is competition in school to get good grades, if everyone in a class gets 100 on every test, then potentially every student can get an A. Once you're out of school, circumstances will change. There are a finite number of jobs, and if more people want jobs than there are jobs to fill, not everyone is going to get the job they want. In some fields today there are more jobs than applicants, and if your field is one of those, then you are almost guaranteed to get a job. But even under such ideal circumstances, some of those jobs will be better than others. Some will pay more. Some will require longer commutes. Some will offer more opportunities for advancement or more stock options. So even if you are sure to get a job, to get the best possible one will require more on your part than just filling out an application.

SPREADING THE WORD

In my experience, the absolute best way of getting whatever you want is to tell everybody you know. As a college student you may not think you have that many contacts, but once you include your family, especially the contacts of your parents, you would be surprised at how many you do have. And then there are the contacts that you don't even know about.

Case: Tod

To earn money while he was in college, Tod worked as a waiter at a fancy restaurant. After graduation, and still looking for a job in his field of communications, he decided to use his position as a waiter as a platform to finding a full-time job. He tried to be as pleasant and helpful as he could to every customer, and if they complimented him for his efforts, he would let them know that he was looking for employment. Two weeks went by without a single lead, and then he hit the jackpot with one table of diners. One of the men told him about a drug company that was hiring hundreds of new salespeople, and another man knew of a public relations firm that was also looking for employees.

If Tod had been working in the kitchen, he would never have had such an opportunity. So Tod's case gives you two lessons: speak up, and when selecting a job, think ahead. If you have a choice between jobs, take the one that offers you the most contact with the general public because you never know when you're going to meet someone who might be useful.

TIPS

- Your very first step in looking for a job is to prepare a resume. If someone asks for your resume, you want to be able to respond immediately, which you won't be able to do if you first have to write one. Don't worry if you don't have any prior work experience to put down. People understand that students won't have a long track record and so even baby-sitting experience is acceptable. If you're getting a personal recommendation for a job from a friend or family member, the most important item on your resume will be where you can be reached.

- When networking, try to be as specific as possible. Saying you are looking for a job isn't enough. You have to be able to tell people what type of job you are seeking, when you would be available, how much money you want, so they can be of most help.

- Remember that if you get a job on a personal recommendation, your performance will reflect on the person who recommended you.

TIPS

- If you're recommended for a job that you think you are going to hate, and maybe quit after the first week, the better choice is not to take it. On the other hand, if you find a job on your own, you don't have to be as concerned about appearances and can take a gamble, knowing that if you hate it, you can leave with a clear conscience.

TO THINE OWN SELF BE TRUE

I offer my advice to people all day long, so I am certainly someone who approves of advice giving. While you should always politely listen to the advice people give you, that doesn't mean you always have to accept it. People may mean well, but they don't necessarily know what's best for you. Where this can be especially difficult is when the advice comes from your parents. They do know you very well, and have spent many years giving you orders, so if you really disagree with them, that can lead to some friction.

Q. My father is a lawyer. His father was a lawyer, and he expects me to become a lawyer too. The only problem is that I can't stand the thought of being cooped up in an office all day. I want to get a job where I can be outdoors. How do I tell my father I'm not going to continue this tradition?

A. Since your father is a lawyer, I suggest you prepare your case very carefully. It's not enough to tell him you don't want to work in an office. Since he's paying for your college, he deserves to hear a more specific plan. After all, you're certainly not going to college in order to become a cab driver. So you have to lay out for your father a career path that will lead to a good job, one that requires a college degree but allows you to roam around outdoors.

Another benefit of mapping out this plan is that it will

clarify in your own mind what type of career you would like for yourself. If you had written to me to say you wanted to be a marine biologist and spend your time diving into the sea, that would be one thing. But you don't seem to have a plan other than to work away from an office. The fact is, nobody particularly likes working in an office, except on cold rainy days maybe, but that's just the place where most business is conducted. Now if you became a trial lawyer, you would get opportunities to work in a courtroom, so you could still be a lawyer but not find yourself in an office all the time. So try to come up with a game plan that you feel comfortable with, and is also practical. (For example, marine biologists have a hard time finding work in their field.) When you have it in place, then you should speak to your father.

Some parents try to live their lives again through their children. For example, if a father didn't make the football team, he'll try to push his son into being a football player (and if he has only a daughter, he may even try to get her to play the game). This can carry through right into adulthood, so that parents can push their offspring toward following their footsteps or in a direction they wish they had taken.

This doesn't have to be negative. For example, if your parents didn't go to college and they pushed you to work harder in high school so you would get the chance to go, that's clearly a good thing. And if they've seen several of their friends' children do very well as accountants, then their motivation in wanting you to become an accountant is also well-meaning. But what if you loathe working with numbers? It's okay for them to make suggestions, but as the person who is going to work at this job for fifty years or so, you get the final say.

On the other hand, you must take a good hard look at yourself. Some young people decide they want to pursue a certain career when they are ten years old, stick to their dream, and enjoy a lifetime working at a career they love. But many other college-age students don't really know what they want. Over the years they may have chosen many different career paths, turning 180 degrees around from one year to the next. If the latter description fits you, be careful not to dismiss your parents' opinions so quickly. Since you're likely to change your mind several times during your college years, their view of what you might be good at could have some validity. I'm not saying you need to obey them. All I'm saying is that it would be a mistake for you to have a negative attitude to a suggested career path just because it comes from your parents. The fact that you share genes and that they raised you does have an impact on how you turned out, so their insights are worth considering.

BLOOD IS THICKER THAN WATER

This saying doesn't have to apply only to family. Any connection you may have to another person can sometimes be put to good advantage, so that fellow classmates, alumni of the same college, friends, friends of friends, all can be useful at some point in your life.

I know that this country was built on rugged individualism and there are those people who say that they don't want anybody's help. I wonder how much of that attitude comes from their inclination toward not wanting to help others. Whatever the motivation, too much rugged individualism can have negative effects. Just because someone recommends you for a job doesn't mean they're going to do it for you. The bulk of the responsibility will always fall on your shoulders. So you'll owe someone a favor because they gave you a leg up. That's not such a tremendous debt, and if you, in turn, do favors for other people, in the long run you'll come out way ahead.

When it comes to contacting alumni, you must talk to the advisers in your college placement office. Some alumni feel strongly about hiring graduates of their college, and these advisers can clue you in and tell you how to contact them. Just blindly writing to everyone in the alumni directory is not going to bear much fruit.

WORKING FOR PARENTS

There is one cautionary note I must include here about working directly for your parents. Sometimes this can work out well, but it can also turn out very badly. Some parents can never see their children as being capable of running a business. They remember all those times you spilled milk at the dinner table, or whatever, and can't change that image in their mind. In those situations, there's nothing the now grown-up child can do to atone for those early "sins." If you're continually treated like a child, rather than an employee, you're going to be miserable.

Some offspring go out on their own, in order to prove their worth to their parents, and then go into the family business with a lot more respect. Depending on the outcome of this foray into the great wide world, this option can be a good solution to the problem.

Just keep in mind that family dynamics can be very complicated. If you are at all uncertain about going into a family business, don't hesitate to see a counselor. It may take someone outside of the situation to properly assess it. The advice you get from an impartial observer could be very valuable.

STRIKE WHILE THE IRON IS HOT

I came to the United States to visit my uncle in San Francisco. After crossing the Atlantic by boat, I planned to stay a few days visiting New York before pushing on to the West Coast. I didn't speak very much English, so when I found out there was a German language newspaper in New York, I bought a copy. In it I read that the New School for Social Research had scholarships available for victims of the Holocaust. Since I was orphaned by the Holocaust, I certainly fit the bill, and so I applied, was accepted, and ended up spending the rest of my life in this country.

You can never know what opportunities may come your way. If you go through life wearing blinders like a horse, so that you can only see directly in front of you, then you will no doubt miss out on a lot of what life has to offer. It's often the zigs and the zags that make life interesting and that lead you to the path of success. Of course some of those zigs and zags can also cause you a lot of trouble. In fact, you might think that someone like me, who lost her entire family to the Holocaust, would be very fearful of change and want to follow a very straight and narrow path. Certainly some people who run into tragedy do just that. Luckily I wasn't raised that way and so I was able to bounce back. And still today, I am always looking for new adventures. I still go skiing. If I'm offered a trip to some far-off land that I've never visited, I jump at the chance. Some of the very best things that have happened to me arose because I was willing to take a risk, and I suggest that you be the same way.

Here's another personal example, even more relevant to the subject of this chapter. I was an assistant professor at Cornell University/ New York Hospital's human sexuality program. A call came through asking for someone to speak to a group of radio community affairs managers. Because there was no fee offered, no one wanted to bother going, but I saw it as an opportunity to fly a trial balloon. I told those managers that now that we had all of this new information about good sexual functioning, they had an obligation to help propagate this material. To make a long story short, that's how I got my own radio show and became Dr. Ruth.

So don't ever be shortsighted. Don't be too lazy to volunteer. Don't be afraid to try something new. You can't expect that every time you do an about-face your fortunes are going to soar. We all make mistakes and I can guarantee that you will too. But if you always play it safe and never take any chances, I can also guarantee that you'll miss out on experiences that might have made a big difference to your life.

Of course I'm not suggesting that it's okay to shoot heroin or play Russian roulette or have unprotected casual sex. Whatever risk-taking you do has to be within reason, but just as you should avoid taking extreme risks, you should also not try to live your life completely risk free.

TIPS

- If you always say no when people ask you to help out, then eventually they'll stop asking, and you may miss out on some very rewarding experiences. If you're really too busy, that's one thing, but if you don't have any plans, say yes to their requests. You never know what might develop.

- If a project presents itself to you, don't be concerned with how much work it will require or time it will take. Instead, look at the upside. Who will you be working with? Will they be interesting people? What will you learn if you take on this assignment? Will it be intellectually challenging?

- If you compare the life of a college student to that of a working parent, you can imagine that you have a lot more free time on your hands. Don't waste it by being bored. If those words ever cross your lips, then immediately go out and do something constructive. You will regret the time you wasted in your youth, and while you can't get back any time you've already wasted, you can limit the amount of future hours that get carelessly discarded.

THE PERSONAL INTERVIEW

Once you've used your contacts to get your foot in the door, and sent along your resume to give your prospective employer the facts he or she needs to know about you, your next job is going to be selling yourself.

Even though you're the person who knows you best, convincing someone else how great you are, or even just that you are right for a particular job, is not easy. I don't think there's anyone who goes in for such an interview without butterflies in their stomach. What you have to remember is that they're only butterflies, not killer bees.

Very rarely do I prepare a speech when I'm giving a lecture. I've done it enough times that I can count on myself to come up with entertaining thoughts to fill that hour. But I'm never up there all by myself. I've got little helpers who are always with me to fill in the rough spots. Who are they? They're the little stories I always weave into my lecture that I know from experience will get a laugh or some other reaction from my audience. You need some of those little helpers that can accompany you to any interviews if you are going to be successful.

Don't think that because you're still young you don't have enough personal experiences to help you out. In fact, you probably have hundreds, though if you're nervous, there's no way you are going to be able to sort through them to find just the right one that's going to help you answer a particular question. But if you work on it, you can probably find two or three with enough universal qualities that you can fit them in when answering almost any question.

What types of stories work best? First there are the moments of crisis. Somebody was sick or you were in an accident or you got lost. As long as the incident shows your ingenuity, it can be used to prove that you are "up to the task," whatever that may be.

You should also look through whatever papers you have written, particularly if you got a good grade. Select one or two with topics that could apply to different subjects and reread them so they're fresh in your mind. If you got an A-plus, you could even offer to send the interviewer a copy.

Lessons your parents taught you can be good fodder for a conversation. There's a good chance that the person who's interviewing you is a parent, but even if they're not, any adult will appreciate the respect you show toward your parents by telling this story.

You should also go back through your life and look for things you did that show off certain qualities you can assume an employer will want to discover about you. For example, if you showed initiative in some way, or proved yourself particularly responsible, or were able to think fast on your feet, or handled a complex task, or showed off a particular skill.

One important fact to bear in mind is that interviewers don't expect a college student to be able to offer a story about how they saved their company from bankruptcy. They'll be lenient when judging how the content of the story applies to the question; instead they'll be jud-

ging you by your delivery. So the more you've practiced your stories
and made them sound interesting, the better you'll appear during the
interview.

And speaking of practice, I would advise you to go on as many interviews as possible. If companies are coming to your college to conduct interviews, sign yourself up as soon as you are allowed. You may
not want to work for some of the first companies you interview with,
but the practice will be very worthwhile. And you might even be surprised to learn that you fit in well with one of these companies and
have a future with them.

A ROLLING STONE GATHERS NO MOSS

I am often asked where I get all my energy. If I had a definite answer,
I could certainly sell it for not just millions, but billions. Some of it
may just be a part of my genes, and that's not something that I can
pass on to you. But some of it is definitely psychological, and so I do
have some ideas I'd like to give you.

One very important source of energy is a positive attitude, although no one can be positive 100 percent of the time. There's always
some incident or some person that's going to get under your skin.
The question is, how long do you allow it to stay there? Now when a
person of a certain age can't remember a name or a date, it's called a
senior moment, and once in a while I have one of those. But the fact
that I don't remember who did what to me I prefer to call a blessing.
I may have a vague feeling about someone, but it doesn't click until
one of my staff reminds me what that person did to me. Holding a
grudge only hurts the person who is holding it. Each of those grudges
holds you down and saps your strength, so if you can let go of them
quickly and completely, you'll have more positive energy.

Another trick of mine is taking naps. I can fall asleep almost anywhere, and even ten minutes of shuteye can do you a world of good.
People who travel with me often find themselves struggling to keep
up with me when we get to our destination. The reason is that I fall
asleep as soon as I strap that seat belt on in the plane, and wake up

raring to go. If my travel partner didn't sleep, then he or she is in trouble.

I also refuse to use the word "tired" or let people around me use it. You can talk yourself into being tired if you say it often enough. On the other hand, if you ban it from your vocabulary, it has much less of an effect on you. Let me give you an example. Let's say I took the red-eye from Los Angeles to New York, landing at 6 A.M., and went right to my office for a meeting. Then I continued to run around seeing clients and jumped on another plane in the afternoon to go give a lecture at a college. I have a perfectly legitimate excuse to drag myself to that lecture hall and tell everyone I'm exhausted. And if I thought about it, I might actually feel tired. But I refuse to even think that word. I go there with the attitude that I'm going to have a good time, and almost every time I do. If I like the students who are running the event and they ask me if I'd like to go out with them after the lecture, I'll go and it never even crosses my mind what kind of day I've had. If it's something I want to do, I just go ahead and do it. On the other hand, even if I've had a fairly quiet day and I go to some black tie affair and it's boring, then I'll find any excuse I can to leave. There's nothing more likely to make you tired than boredom.

TIPS

- If you can't get the people around you to stop complaining about how tired they always are, hang out with some new people who have more energy. There's no reason why you should sit around being bored just because they are boring.

- A positive attitude often brings positive results. Whatever the assignment, if you don't begin by dreading it, the more likely that it won't be as awful as you first thought.

- Push negative thoughts aside with positive ones. I keep a rainy-day file with letters and articles that always bring a smile to my face when I read them. If I'm feeling a bit down, I open that file and keep reading until my sunny disposition is back to its old self.

CONCLUSION

For the arrival of the new millennium, I was asked to write a little piece about the future for a newspaper. As I thought about what to say, it came to me that the future is a lot different from what it used to be. A few hundred years ago, your future was almost totally mapped out for you the day you were born. If you were born to peasant parents, then you would always be a peasant working in the fields. And if you were born into a noble family, just about everything you did was also already settled ahead of time, even whom you were going to marry. Oh, certainly there would be some surprises, but unless some catastrophe befell you, in general your life would be very predictable.

That's not true anymore at all, at least for people living in advanced countries. Computers have wiped out certain job categories, and yet there are more jobs being created than ever before. The consistency of past eras is gone and there's no way to determine what shifts society will go through that will cause your life to twist and turn in response. In fact, the best prediction one could make is that you are going to have to reinvent yourself several times in the course of your lifetime.

The biggest conclusion we can draw from this roller-coaster ride of a future is that a college degree is more important than ever. Sure you read about billionaires who don't have a degree, but they're the exception. The vast majority of people who did not go to college are stuck at the bottom rungs of the ladder. You may not be able to predict your future, but you do want to give yourself the most opportunities possible. Going to college is the best way of doing that.

GOING FOR HELP

If you've read this book, I know that getting that degree is part of your master plan, so I don't really have to sell you on the idea. But while you will hit a few bumps along the way—they're inevitable—what I would hate to see happen is that you come across some hill that you think you can't climb and so you don't finish your education. If that does happen, I want you to go for help. I've given you lots of tips and advice in this book, but I obviously couldn't cover every situation. And even my wisdom will not always be enough to get you through every crisis. Sometimes you require help that is based on the specifics of your problem. That help is probably available at your college. And if it's not, then there are other avenues open to you either in the local community, a bit farther away in a big city, or in your hometown. If you can't go it alone, go for help. Don't allow yourself to drown when there are plenty of people near by with life preservers. They can't reach out to you unless you ask them to because they don't know who is in trouble and who isn't. But they have the training and the experience to help people work through a crisis. If you need their expertise, ask them for it.

MISCELLANEOUS

You might think that, given an entire book, I could cover all bases, but I do have a few other thoughts that didn't fit into any particular chapter. I'd like to pass them on, in no special order.

If your college has a program that allows you to take some courses abroad, I suggest you do so. Two-week vacations to other countries will give you a flavor, but only by living in a foreign country can you really experience it fully. Once you start working, get married, and have a family, such opportunities will become rare. Take advantage of them now and you'll see that it will turn out to be quite a learning opportunity.

Don't be afraid to transfer colleges. If you're not happy where you are, or if you decide you need courses to follow a particular career path that your college doesn't offer, apply to other schools that may be better suited to your needs. Don't allow inertia to keep you some place where you don't belong.

Be very careful about student loans. You may have been taught about the benefit of compound interest in regard to saving money for your future, but it works the other way when borrowing money. If you borrow money for a long time, the interest will add up quickly and you'll end up paying back two or three times the amount you borrowed. That means if you borrow $50,000, you could be paying the bank more than $100,000 by the time you're finished. Student loans may be unavoidable, but think carefully before you go into such large amounts of debt. In the long run you might be better off going to a school near your home where you can live with your parents, or going to a state school instead of a private one. Borrowing large sums should be done only after very careful consideration.

And finally, another lesson from my life. When I was in my early fifties, I was an associate professor teaching human sexuality courses at Brooklyn College. I loved what I was doing and, between that and my private practice as a sex therapist, I thought the path was pretty much set for the rest of my life. Then I did not get rehired for the next academic year at Brooklyn College, and I wondered what would happen to me. Because of that one lecture I gave to those radio community affairs managers, without any warning or planning on my part, I became the celebrated Dr. Ruth.

This lesson teaches that it is never too late. I believe this so much that I once had a television program with that name. That show was aimed at older audiences to let them know they shouldn't give up on life just because they had gray hair and a few wrinkles. But the principles apply to every age group. If you are active and take part in everything that life has to offer, anything is possible. Opportunities will come your way, and you just have to be alert enough to grab them.

So whether it's your grade point average that needs elevating, or a roommate situation that could be improved, or your love life that's scraping along the bottom, don't give up. Just keep trying as hard as you can. Even if you can't predict what the outcome will be, you will definitely reap valuable rewards.

ABOUT THE AUTHORS

Dr. Ruth K. Westheimer is a psychosexual therapist who helped to pioneer the field of media psychology. Her media career began on radio in 1980 with "Sexually Speaking," a program that was syndicated across the country. She has hosted numerous television programs, including "The Dr. Ruth Show" and "Ask Dr. Ruth." She has also appeared on almost every national talk show, including *The Today Show, The Tonight Show, David Letterman,* and *Conan O'Brien.* Her syndicated newspaper column circles the globe, and she has been featured in every major magazine, including on the cover of *People* and *TV Guide.*

Currently Dr. Westheimer is an adjunct professor at New York University. She has also taught at Lehman College, Brooklyn College, Adelphi University, Columbia University, and West Point. She is a fellow of the New York Academy of Medicine and has her own private practice. She frequently lectures at universities across the country and has twice been named "College Lecturer of the Year." She has lectured at more than two hundred college campuses including Harvard, MIT, Princeton, Columbia, Brown, Notre Dame, UCLA, UNC, Johns Hopkins, Georgia Tech, Texas A&M, USC, and Trinity College. She is the author of eighteen books, including *Sex for Dummies, The Value of Family,* and *Grandparenthood.* She has her own Web site on AOL (www.drruth.com) and files reports in streaming video on foreign TV.com. Dr. Westheimer resides in Manhattan and has two children and three grandchildren.

Pierre Lehu has been Dr. Westheimer's "Minister of Communications" for the past nineteen years. He is the co-author of *Dr. Ruth Talks about Grandparents* and the forthcoming *Rekindling Romance for Dummies*. A graduate of New York University (B.A. and M.B.A.), he resides in Brooklyn and is married with two children, one of whom currently is in college.